IN THE STEPS OF
St Patrick

IN THE STEPS OF St Patrick

BRIAN DE BREFFNY

Photographs by George Mott

with 40 illustrations, line drawings and maps

THAMES AND HUDSON

First published in the USA in 1982 by Thames and Hudson, Inc., 500 Fifth Avenue, New York, New York 10110

Library of Congress Catalog Card Number 81-52924

Printed and bound in Great Britain

Contents

I
Patrick's Romano-British Background

It is in the Christian society of late Roman Britain that we must seek the origin and cultural background of Magonus Succatus Patricius, better known as Patrick, Ireland's patron saint, the Apostle of Ireland. This we know from that tantalizingly brief autobiographical testimony written by Patrick in Latin and known as the *Confessio*.

In the *Confessio* Patrick informs us that he was the son of one Calpurnius, a deacon, who was the son of the late Potitus, a priest. At the time of Patrick's birth, in the latter years of the fourth century, or early in the fifth, the clergy were not required to remain celibate.

Archaeological and epigraphical evidence attest the spread of Christianity in Britain prior to the Edict of Milan in 313, but before that date, Christian worship had had to be more or less clandestine because of the attitude of the Roman authorities, which ranged from official indifference at some periods to active persecution of Christians at others. Septimus Severus, the Emperor who reigned from 193 to 211, campaigned in Britain during the last two years of his reign and attempted then to supress proselytization by ordering the penalty of death for converts to Christianity. It was probably at that time that the soldier Alban, a Roman citizen, was beheaded, becoming Britain's first recorded Christian martyr. He had been converted to Christianity by a priest whom he had sheltered in his house in the tribal city of Verulamium, later named St Albans in his honour.

Another period of fierce persecution was inflicted on the Christians in Britain during the reign of the Emperor Trajan Decius, 249–51. It was probably at that time that two Christian soldiers. Aaron and Julius, died for their faith in the legionary fortress at Caerleon in South Wales where the Roman Legion II Augusta was stationed. The need for secrecy among the Christian communities in Britain in the third century is suggested by two acrostic word-squares, one found in the plaster of the wall of a Romano-British house at Cirencester in Gloucestershire, another on a pottery vessel discovered at Manchester. These apparently innocent graffiti were, in fact, cryptograms containing the letters of the word 'Paternoster' in the form of a cross, and prefaced and terminated by the letters A and Ω to recall Christ's words, 'I am the Alpha and the Omega, the First and the Last, the Beginning and the End.'

The conversion of the Emperor Constantine heralded a new era for Christians throughout the Roman Empire. Constantine, who had been acclaimed as Emperor by the army at York in Britain in 306, was not, in fact, baptized until the end of his life, long after his actual conversion, but he ascribed his extraordinary success to his commitment to Christianity and the support of the Christian God. The Edict of Milan in 313 granted toleration to Christians in the Roman Empire, and restored to them personal and corporate property which had been seized during the persecutions.

Within a year of the Edict of Milan, bishops from London and York attended the Council of Arles. The presence of several British bishops at the Council of Rimini in 359 indicates that, by that date, the ecclesiastical administration had expanded and there was some organized structure within the Church in Britain. Christianity, which had found its first neophytes mainly among the poorer inhabitants of the towns, now made progress in almost every class of British society, despite the persistence of earlier pagan cults and occasional spurts of pagan revival.

This, then, was the religious background of Patrick's family. We do not know at what date his ancestors were converted to Christianity, but his grandfather, the priest Potitus (who was apparently already deceased at the time of Patrick's birth), must be placed around the middle of the fourth century, when British bishops went to Rimini.

A second document from Patrick's pen, the *Letter to Coroticus,* provides the additional information that Patrick's father held a post in the Roman administration; he was a *decurion.*

In the earliest years of Britain as a Roman province, all but the independently ruled tribal areas of the country was under the direct rule of a Roman governor. Subsequently, self-governing communities emerged, towns of a certain status which attained the rank of a *colonia.* The autonomy of a colonia rested in a local government modelled on that of Rome itself, with a constitution and a council corresponding to the Roman Senate called the *ordo.* This council was composed of about one hundred leading citizens, the *decuriones.* A prominent native or resident qualified to serve as a decurion on the grounds of his civil status and property-ownership.

Originally a decurion was elected to that office by the assembly of citizens, but by the time of the Emperor Diocletian at the close of the third century, the ordo had become a virtually self-perpetuating body, and eventually the office of decurion became hereditary. So it was, therefore, at the end of the fourth century when Patrick's father, the deacon Calpurnius, held this rank.

While the decurion might enjoy financial advantages accruing from his office, such as obtaining lucrative leases of state concessions, the office also imposed onerous duties and financial obligations. The decurion was responsible for preparing the annual taxation budget, and he had to share the cost of his town's public entertainments which, if it had a theatre, would have included plays, farces, recitations and mimes, as well as gladiatorial contests, bull-baiting, bear-baiting and cock-fighting in the amphitheatre. The decurion was also responsible for the maintenance of public services such as the heating system of the public baths, the cleaning of the latrines and the sweeping of the streets. Moreover, after Diocletians' reforms, the decurion became personally responsible for the taxes of defaulters.

The burdens of the office often outweighed its advantages, so frequently men of decurion families sought exemption from service, especially if they feared that it might lead them to bankruptcy. For a rich man, one means of exemption was to buy his way into the equestrian order, a higher social class. Another means of escaping service as a decurion was ordination to the priesthood. It is in that context that we may see Patrick's immediate family in the latter half of the fourth century. They were a family of standing in their own community, enjoying privileges, and with the hereditary obligation of service as decurions in their local administration. Patrick's grandfather, the priest, may have taken holy orders to avoid having to serve as a decurion, while Patrick's father was a deacon in the ecclesiastical establishment and a decurion in the civil establishment.

Patrick's family did not, however, belong to an important colonia but, as he tells us in the *Confessio*, to a '*vicus*', which was a lesser administrative unit. While the colonia had consisted of Roman citizens, administrative regions had developed among the native British population also, frequently based on the pre-Roman tribal divisions. The principal town of the region became its administrative centre, called by the Romans the *civitas*. It had an organ of local government similar to the colonia, with men of substance of the place serving, according to the Roman system, in the offices of magistrate and decurion. Long before Patrick's time, any real distinction between a colonia and a civitas had been swept away by the Emperor

Caracalla's *Constitutio Antoniana* of 212, which had extended Roman citizenship to all free-born subjects in the Roman provinces. The 'vicus' of which Patrick wrote was a lesser administrative unit than the civitas.

Below the level of the civitas there were two lesser units, the vicus and the *pagus*, but while the pagus, a grouping of inhabitants of a rural area, had no form of local government of its own, the vicus had a local council like that of the civitas, save that the vicus usually had only one pair of magistrates, instead of the senior pair and the junior pair of the civitas.

The term 'vicus' was used in Rome itself for a subdivision of the city. In Britain, however, the term was applied to the smaller town or settlement which grew up around the establishment of a military fort as it attracted traders and other camp-followers. A vicus might grow into a town of some importance, like Petuaria at Brough-on-Humber.

Patrick's *Confessio* actually names the vicus to which his father belonged. In the Paris Manuscript of the *Confessio* the place appears as 'bannavem taburniae', but in all the other early manuscript texts it is 'bannavem taberniae'. It seems that this must be read either as 'Bannaventa Berniae' or 'Banna Venta Berniae'. This place has often been referred to as Patrick's birthplace, but he does not imply in the *Confessio* that this was necessarily his own place of birth, but rather that it was the town to which his father belonged, the actual text-words describing Calpurnius being 'quid fuit vico bannavem taberniae'. As the place-name is in the ablative case here, it is quite clear that Patrick was not using vicus to mean a quarter or a street of the place, as has sometimes been suggested, but rather that the place itself was of the category called a vicus. Patrick goes on in the *Confessio* to explain that his father owned a *villula* near the vicus. By 'villula' we may understand a small villa, the country estate of the family.

In the towns of Roman Britain which have been excavated, scant evidence has been found of spacious or luxurious housing for those prominent citizens who would have served on the town council in the office of decurion. It has been inferred, therefore, that most of them, who would have been prosperous landowners, had as their principal abode a villa on their country estate, rather than in the town to which they belonged. John Wacher estimates that there must have been at least two thousand decurions in Britain at any one time, but only about six hundred Romano-British villas of all types have as yet been identified. Some of these villas were luxurious, the amenities of the dwelling-house itself including a heating-system, and the principal rooms being embellished with mosaic floors and painted frescoes, Outside the dwelling-house, the finer villa had a courtyard and gardens as well as a barn and other out-buildings.

Patrick tells us in the *Letter to Coroticus* that there were both male and female slaves at his father's country estate. As slavery was a part *p. 22* of the established social system of the Roman Empire, it is not surprising that the decurion Calpurnius should have owned slaves, but knowing of their presence on Patrick's family's estate helps us to visualize the 'villula' where he was living at the time of his abduction. The house of a member of the governing class, it may well have been a gracious dwelling with some pretensions to style and comfort. While the poorer country people in Britain during the Roman period inhabited primitive round dwellings, with mud or wattle walls supporting a roof of turf or thatch, the residences of the upper classes were sophisticated buildings which reached their zenith of luxury in the fourth century.

How then can we picture the country house where Patrick lived? The principal rooms of the Romano-British villa were colourfully decorated, the wall-paintings on plaster generally executed in red, olive-green and brown. Sometimes the ceiling was painted too, as in a villa at Verulamium where a ceiling was decorated with yellow doves on a purplish background.

In some villas which have been excavated, the principal rooms had mosaic floors. The design of these floors ranged from a simple pattern to scenes drawn mainly from the repertoire of classical mythology, such as the mosaic floor of the *frigidarium* of a villa excavated at Low Ham in Somerset, which depicts Dido and Aeneas. With the spread of Christianity certain mythological scenes were given a Christian connotation as well. On the floors of villas known to have been owned by Christians the scene of Bellerophon killing the Chimaera has been found, seemingly used to illustrate the triumph of good over evil.

The villa which has been excavated at Lullingstone, Kent, was owned by Christians. In the apse of what was presumably the dining-room is a mosaic depicting the abduction of Europa by Zeus in the guise of a bull, and another of Bellerophon riding the winged horse Pegasus and killing the Chimaera, between roundels which depict the four seasons and panels with a geometric design. Adjacent to that room are rooms which were used for Christian worship, as is proclaimed by a prominent Chi-Ro monogram above the decorative painted colonnade. (The Chi-Ro monogram comprised the first two letters of Christ's name in Greek.) The bays of the colonnade are painted with richly-costumed figures standing with their arms up-

lifted in the attitude of prayer of early Christianity. Possibly these orantes represented the villa-owner and his family.

Again, in a villa excavated at Hinton St Mary, Dorset, mosaics with both pagan and Christian motifs were discovered. A Chi-Ro *p. 6* symbol identifies the portrait bust in a floor as Christ, while another mosaic depicts Bellerophon slaying the Chimaera.

The site of the country estate of Patrick's father, the decurion Calpurnius, has not been identified, but as Patrick described the villa with the diminutive 'villula', we may conclude that it was not one of the larger and grander villas, and it may well not have boasted such rich decoration as the Lullingstone villa or the Hinton St Mary villa, whose owners must have been very wealthy men. It would be wrong, nevertheless, to assume that even a modest country house of the period would not have been comfortable. Indeed, the standard of comfort achieved in Romano-British villas of the fourth century was not to be repeated until the nineteenth century. Many villas had a sophisticated bath system; some relatively small villas of the middle of the fourth century had a communicating bath-suite. The rooms of the Romano-British villa were sparsely, but often elegantly furnished. The legs of a table from one Dorset villa, for instance, were shaped in the form of an animal with carved head and feet and bowed chest. The usual items of household furniture were woven basket chairs and couches, often with well-padded mattresses, folding stools, three-legged tables, cupboards and caskets. Cooking was done on a charcoal fire over which pots and pans were placed on a grid-iron. The well-equipped kitchen had a variety of cooking vessels, a pestle, a mortar, knives, choppers, pastry-cutters. The rooms were lit by candelabra or by terracotta oil-lamps, and warmed by a portable charcoal-burning brazier.

Hundreds of thousands of words have been expended in defence of one theory or another concerning the location in Britain of Patrick's family's country house, where he was living at the age of sixteen when he was abducted by Irish raiders. The question remains unsolved, and various theories still have their faithful supporters. Even though modern scholarship has served to dismiss some long-cherished theories, they have not been abandoned. One such theory would have it that Patrick's home was in Scotland. We can be sure that this was not so because the area north of Hadrian's Wall did not, in Patrick's time, have a Roman style administration, and as we know that Patrick's father was a decurion he must have lived in a region where the Roman-style administration obtained. In 365-7 the Scots and Picts who attacked Britain wrested the area north of Hadrian's Wall from Roman control. Count Theodosius was dispatched from Gaul to restore order, and the control of the barbarian inhabitants beyond the frontier-line was entrusted to pro-Roman native chieftians who acted as *praefecti gentium*. The home of the decurion Calpurnius could not, therefore, have been beyond the frontier. Nevertheless, one may still hear today a Parish Priest in Ireland informing his flock from the pulpit on St Patrick's Day that their national apostle was a native of Scotland.

Where, then, should we look for the town (vicus) of 'Bannavem Taberniae' and the nearby country estate of Patrick's family? It must have been not far from the western seaboard of Britain, in a region subject to the depredations of raiding parties coming from across the Irish sea. This suggests the Severn estuary, the Welsh coast, or the coastal regions of Lancashire, Westmorland or Cumberland.

There was, in fact, a place in Roman Britain named 'Bannaventa' whose name could be taken to be the 'Bannavem Taberniae' or 'Bannaventa Berniae' of the *Confessio*, but it is in quite the wrong part of Britain. The site of this Bannaventa was Whilton Lodge near Daventry in Northamptonshire, on Watling Street, beyond Lactodorum, now Towcester, the third station on that important route. It is mentioned in the *Antonine Itinerary*, an official route-list compiled in the early third century, and in the fourth century it was selected and developed as a stronghold for the protection of the communication network and imperial supplies; from Bannaventa a spur-road branched off to a metal-working centre at Duston. Bannaventa was just the sort of community which grew into a small commercial town around a military installation and became an administrative vicus.

Because the name of this Romano-British site Bannaventa was known, it was quickly seized upon as 'Bannaventa Berniae'. The Daventry area still has its determined partisans, who claim that this was the home of Patrick's family. It is, however, too far from the scene of Irish raids. Is it conceivable that a party of Irish raiders would have risked penetrating deep into the centre of Britain to capture and carry off slaves and booty? A site in the southern midlands of Britain, far from the western coast, must be discounted.

Already in the seventh century, two hundred years after Patrick's death, there was doubt about the site of 'Bannavem Taberniae'. Muirchú, Patrick's biographer, writing at that time, stated that he had 'discovered for certain and beyond doubt' that the place in question was 'Ventre'. Muirchú does not tell us how he discovered this, or why he was certain beyond doubt. In his time there were a number of manuscript biographies of Patrick in circulation. Muirchú's source may have been one or more of these, or oral tradition, or both. The place known in Muirchú's time as 'Ventre', and which he was sure was Patrick's birthplace, was the Romano-British Venta Silurum, now Caerwent, Gwent.

Venta Silurum was a walled town with bastions, closely built-up, and with a stone-built amphitheatre. It was not a very large town, but it was an important one, a tribal city which functioned as a cantonal capital. It was therefore a 'civitas' and not a 'vicus', and so cannot be the town of Patrick's father, referred to in the *Confessio*. There is no doubt that Venta Silurum was a civitas; that it was so is testified by an inscription describing the commissioning local council as 'Ordo Reipublicae Civitatis Silurum'. There are still partisans, however, of the theory that Patrick came from Caerwent, and it must be admitted that its situation by the Bristol Channel at the estuary of the Severn is a plausible one for Patrick's home, being a region which was vulnerable to raids from Ireland. Other places near Caerwent have also been suggested. Malone has proposed Burrium, now Usk, which is farther inland, and Eoin MacNeill has suggested Gobannium, now Abergavenny, yet farther inland, but both these interpretations present etymological and paleographical difficulties and have little in their favour.

Some researchers have tried to pinpoint Patrick's place of origin by considering the whereabouts of churches with an early dedication to St Patrick, but it is likely that a cult of Patrick in these places is due to the missionary activities of Irish monks. There are four early dedications to St Patrick in Wales, two in Yorkshire, two in Cumberland, three in Westmorland, one in Northumberland.

Banna, a fort-site at Bewcastle near Birdoswald, is another place which has been suggested as the possible identity of 'Bannavem Taberniae'. Banna is mentioned in the *Ravenna Cosmography* and also in epigraphical sources. Partisans of the theory that this was Patrick's home claim that the last part of the place-name as it appears in the *Confessio* might have been a mis-transcription of *berniciae*, referring to the region north and south of Hadrian's Wall which was known as 'Bernicia'; some have suggested also that the shaft of a seventh-century High Cross in Birdoswald churchyard, fourteen and a half feet in height and sculpted with panels depicting Christ and the Agnus Dei, may have been erected by Irish monks in Northumbria to commemorate Patrick's birthplace two hundred years after his death. However, even if we are to accept 'Banna Berniciae' for 'Bannaventa Berniae', we are left without an explanation for 'venta', and there seems to be no further reason for supposing that this Banna is the place in question, and nothing to show that the High Cross was intended to have any association with Patrick.

A more probable identification of Patrick's home is Clannaventa, a settlement which grew up around a Roman fort at Ravenglass on the coast of Cumberland, highly vulnerable to raids from across the Irish Sea. Clannaventa is mentioned in the early third-century *Antonine Itinerary*, in the *Notitia Dignitatum*, a list of civilian and military outposts throughout the Roman Empire prepared at the end of the fourth century, about the time of Patrick's birth, and in the *Ravenna Cosmography*. Originally a fort, it is exactly the sort of place that would have developed into a vicus, retaining, as it did, its military importance as an outpost over a long period, and being sufficiently far from a civitas to have enjoyed its own administration. The four-acre site is now covered with trees. A bath-house attached to the fort has survived because it was incorporated into a medieval building, and some of its walls are standing, over twelve feet high; in the niches where the bathers left their garments, traces of the original salmon-pink rendering can be seen. At three or four places within a few miles of the fort there have been finds of Roman material.

Was Clannaventa then the vicus of Patrick's father? Did Patrick, as a youth, walk that site, visit that bath-house with his father the decurion? Perhaps. Ravenglass, on the Cumberland coast facing the Isle of Man, at the northern extremity of Roman civilization in Britain and within easy reach of Irish raiders, is just the sort of area where we would expect Patrick's family to have lived, and its remoteness would account for Patrick's rustic Latin which he lamented in his writings. The farmland of the coastal plain on either side of the

River Esk could well have been the site of the 'villula' of Patrick's family, but we have no proof. Moreover, if we are to accept 'Clannaventa' for 'Bannaventa' there would have to have been an error made in transcribing by some early copyist whose version was used by all the later scribes. That could have happened, but how is 'Berniae' to be explained? Père Grosjean has suggested that for 'Bannavem Taberniae' we should understand 'Clannaventa Berniciae', drawing on a reference to Bernicia as in the case of the Bewcastle site; but it seems doubtful whether the region known as Bernicia extended as far south and west as Clannaventa.

Neither Patrick's own name, nor the names of his father and grandfather, offer any clue to help us to identify the family's residence in Roman Britain, for both Calpurnius and Potitus were common names. One particular notable named Calpurnius is commemorated in an inscription in the wall of a vault under the church at Hexham in Northumberland. His full name was 'Q. Calpurnius Concessinus', and it is likely that this inscription was known to one of the seventh-century Irish hagiographers – whence, perhaps, the name of 'Concessa' which we first find attributed to Patrick's mother by his biographer Muirchú who had access to those hagiographical texts. It is possible, on the other hand, that Muirchú got the name Concessa from some oral tradition, or from a source totally unconnected with the Hexham inscription, so this line of enquiry must be considered too fragile to be of value.

Tirechán, writing in the second half of the seventh century and quoting Ultán of Arbraccan, Co. Meath, the Bishop of the Ui Conchobair who died about 657, states that Patrick had four names: Magonus Succatus Patricius Corthirthiacus. The last of these four is, in fact, only a latinization of 'Cothrige' which was an old Irish form of Patricius. By the fourth century the Roman usage was for a citizen to have three names. The first, the '*praenomen*', usually a common name, was frequently abbreviated to its initial letter in inscriptions. The second name, the '*nomen*' or '*nomen gentilicium*', was the person's family or clan name, equivalent to the surname in modern Europe. The third name, the '*cognomen*', which began as an optional extra name to aid in identification, denoted the bearer's trade, a personal achievement or attribute, or even a physical peculiarity.

It would appear that Patrick's full name was Magonus Succatus Patricius, Magonus being his praenomen, and Succatus his nomen gentilicium, the latinization of the British name 'Sucat'. Muirchú recorded this name in his seventh-century biography of the Saint: 'Patrick, who was also called *Sochet*, was of British nationality, born in Britain, the son of the deacon Calpurnius ...' Patricius, meaning 'patrician' or 'aristocrat', would have been Patrick's cognomen.

By the time of Patrick's birth at the end of the fourth century, the entire fabric of the Roman administration, political, social, and military, was enfeebled. Within the next three generations, in Patrick's own lifetime, the whole fabric disintegrated. During the period of confusion, which began at the time of Patrick's childhood and became more intense in the following decades, the governing class, men who held positions like Patrick's father, struggled to maintain the political and social structure of Roman Britain. When they realized that they could not count on help from beleaguered Rome they attempted to preserve order autonomously. They received their first lesson in self-government in 410, when the Emperor Honorius, in answer to a plea for help and protection, informed the British that they would have to look after themselves.

In Patrick's lifetime in the first half of the fifth century the magistrates and decurions in Britain acted as the trustees of Roman order and civilization. They tried, to the best of their ability, to stave off the turmoil caused by barbarian invaders. When St Germanus visited Britain from Gaul in 429 he found the country battered and suffering from the barbarian attacks, although where he stayed, at Verulamium, now St Albans, he remarked that the local government was still carried on by men of the wealthy Romanized British ruling class who dressed richly and enjoyed the adulation of the populace.

Rome had been obliged to withdraw her forces from Britain systematically in order to deploy them on the Continent. Already by 395, the *Notitia Dignitatum* listed as being stationed elsewhere in Europe a number of units which had previously been in Britain. In 402, the Legio VI had to be called back to Italy from York along with the remnants of the Legio II Augusta, to defend the northern Italian frontiers. In 407 the usurper Constantine III, who had been raised to the purple in Britain, took what remained of the army there to Gaul to help repulse the hordes of Vandals and other barbarians who had swept in from the east. The British, left with no alternative defence force or experience of military leadership, became increasingly vulnerable to attacks as the Roman military apparatus was diminished.

Irish raiders like those who abducted Patrick were not the only attackers; the Picts swept down into Britain from the north and the Saxons made incursions by sea from the east. While Patrick's family witnessed the gradual dismantling of the Roman structure, Rome inexorably lost her grip on Britain. The supply of coinage dwindled;

the last issue reached Britain in 435. Practically no Romano-British pottery of the fifth century has come to light, which indicates that the adverse conditions in the country must have brought that industry to a halt.

St Germanus, who had been a soldier in his younger days, helped the British whom he encountered to organize a militia, and led them into battle against the barbarian invaders with the war-cry 'Alleluia'. But this was an isolated instance of organized resistance. Lacking means of defence, the British resorted to the expedient of employing one group of barbarian invaders, the Saxons, to fight the others. This resulted in an increase in the power and strength of the Saxons, who became more deeply entrenched in Britain. In 446, a final desperate appeal came to the Roman authorities on the Continent: 'The barbarians in harassed Britain drive us to the sea, the sea drives us to the barbarians. Between those two modes of death we are either drowned or slaughtered.' But beleaguered Rome was in no position to help. In the latter half of the fifth century what remained of the Roman structure in Britain collapsed, and the marks of Roman civilization in Britain were so completely obliterated that Gildas, writing in the next century, knew nothing of the Roman administrative network that had existed in Britain. In fact, he did not even know that Rome had ruled Britain for several centuries and had effectively Romanized the country.

As the Roman political, social and military orders waned and finally disappeared, the Christian Church emerged from the strife as the spiritual heir of Rome in Britain. Confronted with the problems of diminishing prosperity, and the evanescence of order in their society, the Christian British appear to have sought and found security in the spiritual values of their faith. The work of Fastidius, *On the Christian Life*, written in correct Latin in Britain between about 420 and 430, is an exhortation to the spiritual life composed at this time. It expounded the morality of a simple, leisured, Christian life devoted to piety and charity.

The Pelagian heresy which had begun to trouble the Christian Church early in the fourth century originated in the teaching on grace professed by a cultivated Romano-British layman, Pelagius, who had travelled widely abroad and lived in Italy and in North Africa. Controversy arising from Pelagian doctrine raged in Britain, and in Patrick's lifetime the heresy was widespread there. It was because so many British Christians espoused Pelagian beliefs that Pope Celestine I sent St Germanus over to Britain from Gaul in 429 at the head of a legation to suppress the heresy.

Despite the evidence of Christian activity in Britain at the end of the fourth and in the first half of the fifth century, next to nothing has been found of church buildings of the Romano-British era, while a number of pagan structures have been identified. One urban building excavated that has been identified as a church is a little apsidial building in the civitas named Calleva Atrebatum, a tribal cantonal capital on the site of Silchester, Hampshire. It could have accommodated about fifty worshippers, and was built near the administrative centre of the town. The orientation of this church, with the entrance and narthex to the east and the apse to the west, conforms to Early Christian practice on the Continent. Prior to the fifth century the sacred direction, east, was vested not in the altar but in the portal. This was the plan of the first basilica of St Peter at Rome, and of the Constantinian basilica of the Holy Sepulchre at Jerusalem. In the little Silchester church, two aisles flank the nave which terminates in an apse with transepts.

From the site of the town called Durobrivae at Water Newton, Cambridgeshire, a hoard of Romano-British church plate has been recovered, including a simple two-handled silver chalice and a silver bowl for use in the communion service. Several of the silver objects and a circular gold disc bear the Chi-Ro symbol.

The church in which Patrick and his family worshipped would undoubtedly have been a small building. It may even have been a chapel attached to, or part of, their residence, like the one in the villa at Lullingstone, which had an external entrance so that it could be used by worshippers from outside as well as the inhabitants. However simple its place of assembly, a Romano-British Christian congregation would have had its sacred vessels; those used by Patrick and his family may have been similar to the ones found at Water Newton; they may also have kept votive plaques like those found there: stylized palm leaves of thin silver or silver-gilt.

Silver votive plaques of a similar kind, but associated with pagan worship, have been found, some dating from the fourth century, for example those at the temple site at Maiden Castle in Dorset, and in the north at the fort named Banna, at Bewcastle near Birdoswald in Cumbria – one of the places suggested as Patrick's British home. Certainly pagan cults and pagan worship continued in the latter part of the fourth and in the fifth century in Britain, alongside and in competition with Christian worship.

The official Roman cults had been promoted in Britain after the conquest as part of the policy of Romanization. Temples and altars were built dedicated to Jupiter, Juno and Minerva, the deities of the

Capitoline Triad, and there is abundant evidence of devotion to other deities of the Roman pantheon.

Celtic deitics also had their devotees. At Condercum, now Benwell, Tyne and Wear, a fort on Hadrian's Wall, there was a small temple dedicated to the Celtic divinity Antenociticus, with a sculpted head of the god. Sometimes, in the popular mind, the Roman and Celtic divinities were associated and became syncretized.

One prominent pagan cult which had reached Roman Britain from the Orient and found lodgment there, was the worship of Mithras (above), a vigorous, youthful deity who represented the victory of the soul after death. Five widely distributed Mithraic temples have been identified in Britain.

Undoubtedly Patrick would have been aware of pagan practice in his native country. Many people continued to be attracted to the older forms of worship, and in the *Confessio* Patrick writes of people drawing away from the true God and disobeying the priests. Curse tablets – curses scribbled on metal plaques and invoking pagan deities – were a popular superstition; several such tablets have been found in Britain in the course of excavations. Many readers of the *Confessio* have wondered what was the youthful sin of which Patrick writes, a transgression which he states that he committed in the space of one hour at a time when he did not believe in the living God although he was nominally a Christian. It is tempting to speculate that the sin of the fifteen-year-old Patrick may have been participation in some pagan ritual or invocation of a pagan deity – or, perhaps, a sacrilegious or blasphemous act in his own Christian church.

Patrick describes himself in the *Confessio* as a 'rusticus' – a country fellow, yet we know that he came from a privileged and educated family. Much has been written about the clumsiness of Patrick's Latin, its quaintness, its faulty syntax. As he himself implies in his 'confession', this was due at least in part to his lack of attention to serious matters in his boyhood and youth. And, of course, his abduction into slavery at the age of sixteen would have curtailed any studies which he might have continued in the art of rhetoric. The residence of Patrick's family, too, at the western or north-western edge of Britain, far from such smart towns as Verulamium, must have contributed to the simplicity of his early education. It was years later, after having encountered centres of urban learning and civilization, that Patrick realized how much he was, in reality, a country boy, a greenhorn, by origin, and this he readily admitted.

The Irish had begun to attack the western coast of Britain several decades before Patrick's birth. The 'Verona List' of hostile tribes on the confines of the Roman Empire, compiled about 312-14, includes the Scotti from Ireland. The first recorded attack on Britain from the direction of Ireland dates from the 360s. A series of late-Roman defended sites along the western coastline of Britain indicates that attack from across the Irish Sea was a sufficiently important menace to merit the construction of forts. It is evident that by the time of Patrick's abduction, incursions by raiders from Ireland were not a rarity. Patrick, in the *Confessio*, writes of 'tot milia hominum', 'many thousands', having been taken into captivity in Ireland from Britain like himself. The hoard of Roman silver found at Coleraine, Co. Derry, dateable on numismatic grounds to about 423, must have been the loot brought back by one such raiding party. Another hoard, consisting of hacked-up silver vessels of Roman origin, snatched in Britain and brought back to Ireland, was discovered at Balline, Co. Limerick. Roman gold and silver coins found near the pagan chamber-tomb at New Grange were probably also part of the loot from raids in Britain.

In the *Confessio* Patrick tells us only that he was captured on his father's estate when he was about sixteen years old and taken as a slave to Ireland. He expands on this in his *Letter to Coroticus*, where he speaks of his mission among the Irish, the same race of people who once took him captive and ravaged the slaves and maidservants of his father's house.

Ireland, the country to which he was taken, was a very different country from the one in which he had grown up. Untouched by the refinement of Roman civilization, Ireland had no finely constructed network of roads like those of Roman Britain; no urban life; nothing to compare with the skilfully planned towns in Britain, in some of which, well-spaced houses were sited in gardens alongside a grid-pattern of streets: no theatres, amphitheatres, temples, churches, public buildings or baths. There were no villas with mosaic floors and frescoed walls in Ireland, no lead pipes to carry water; no equestrian statues or handsomely sculpted tombstones. The carpenter's plane, in use in Britain, was not known in Ireland. The Irish agriculturist had not been introduced to the plough – neither to the heavy plough brought into Britain from Gaul before the conquest, nor to the simple, light plough consisting of a coulter to cut the earth and a ploughshare to lift the earth, brought to Britain by the Romans. Ireland had no coinage.

Even though Patrick had lived in a distant, rural region of Roman Britain, the abrupt change the youth encountered in Ireland, not just in his situation as a slave, but in the society, the economy, the whole civilization, must have been both shocking and disconcerting to him.

II
Slavery and Escape

The raid on Patrick's family home was accompanied by acts of brutality and ferocity: an appalling and terrifying experience. In the *Confessio* Patrick tells us that he was then about sixteen, describing himself as a youth, little more than 'a beardless boy'. Many years after the event in referring to the raid in his *Letter to Coroticus*, Patrick chose the verb *devastare*, meaning to lay waste, ravage, or devastate, in describing the behaviour of the raiders to the people on his father's estate. The lad would most probably have been carried away bound or chained, and thrown with other captives into a boat bound for Ireland, a rough sea-crossing to an unknown destination.

What was it like, that Ireland of the early fifth century to which Patrick was brought as a slave? We really know little about that pre-Christian Celtic society other than what we can learn from the excavation of the sites which were inhabited, and from the metal and pottery artefacts which have been found, but these are not numerous. The popular image of chieftains in chariots, of long-robed, long-bearded druids with golden ornaments and boughs of mistletoe, performing ceremonies around mysterious stone circles, has hardly more basis than the romantic imagination of writers of the last century. Their sources were the accounts of Caesar, who described the sacred Celtic sites on the Continent – groves and woods with sacred trees – and the tales of the Irish Celtic heroes, which were not written down until the medieval period. The pre-Christian Irish relied on the memory of their priests and scholars for the oral transmission of their laws, their beliefs and their lore; they left us no contemporary written records. Each Celtic tribe seems to have developed its own cult and local deities, and there is no firm distinction between their gods and their heroes.

Farming was the basic economy of fifth-century Celtic Ireland, predominantly the raising of cattle, sheep and pigs. Single farmsteads were usual. On such a farmstead, the household was composed of a man with his wives, children and grandchildren – the extended joint family with their servants and slaves. The usual homestead of the family group was the type of protected settlement called a ring-fort, referred to colloquially as a *rath,* or sometimes as a *dun*.

The ring-fort was essentially a protected residential site rather than a fort proper. Archaeological surveys indicate that there were as many as thirty or forty thousand ring-forts in Ireland. The residential enclosure was usually about seventy-five feet in diameter, surrounded by one or more banks of earth or stone and ditches, with a causeway up to the gate. Animals could be brought into the enclosure when necessary. Within, there would be a central round dwelling-house of mud and wattle or dry-stone, or perhaps a number of small round dwellings.

Grander, but less numerous than the ring-forts, were fortified sites called hill-forts. These were frequently of several acres, set usually on low, rounded hill-tops overlooking good agricultural land and enclosed by one or more banks and ditches. The smallest known hill-fort is an enclosure of only one acre, the largest is forty acres in extent. These hill-forts were surely tribal centres, the strongholds of chiefs who exercised their sway over the region. It has been estimated that by the fifth century, about one hundred and fifty petty kings or chiefs had emerged in Ireland, and the most important of these would have occupied the hill-forts which have been identified as royal sites – Tara in Co. Meath, Dun Ailinne in Co. Kildare, Eamhain Mhacha (Navan Fort) in Co. Armagh, Clogher in Co. Tyrone, and Cornaskee in Co. Fermanagh. These royal sites were assembly places as well as dwellings. The people also gathered for ceremonies at Rathcroghan

in Co. Roscommon, Tlachtga (the Hill of Ward) and Tailteann (Teltown) in Co. Meath, and on the Hill of Uisneach in Co. Westmeath.

Patrick tells us in the *Confessio* that during his years as a slave he pastured the flocks of his master. How this man acquired Patrick we do not know. In all probability it was by barter of sheep or cattle with the raiders who had brought the lad to Ireland. Patrick relates that he served this master for six years. He does not, however, name him. In Muirchú's *Life of Patrick* we find the man named as Miliucc, and described as 'a certain pitiless pagan king'.

Neither the *Confessio* nor Muirchú names the place of Patrick's captivity, but Tirechán, a second early biographer, who named localities whenever possible, wrote that Patrick's servitude was with 'Miliuc maccu-Boin on the peak of the mountain of Scirit next to the mountain of Miss' (Slemish). Later sources, such as the late ninth- to early tenth-century *Tripartite Life* and the *Lebar Brecc*, describe Miliucc as the king of Dál Araidhe (Dalaradia), which was the name of a region in eastern Ulster. In this region the great plug of rock which forms Slemish rises steeply and dramatically to a height of 1,437 feet above the smooth lava of the Antrim plateau.

The kingdom of Dalaradia is indeed a most likely place for Patrick to have been left as a slave when he was brought over by his captors from Britain, being within easy access of the ports along the north-east coast of Antrim, between the mouth of the Bush and Larne in the kingdom of Dalriada. (The similarity of the names of these two kingdoms, Dalaradia and Dalriada, has often caused confusion.)

There is a strong early tradition of Slemish as the place where Patrick lived as a slave. Miliucc's homestead, according to belief in the region since time immemorial, was a ring-fort on the summit of the Hill of Skerry. An old burial-ground and the ruins of a chapel mark the supposed site. *plate 1*

If, indeed, Slemish was the place of Patrick's captivity, his journey following his escape, of two hundred miles to the port from which he eventually sailed to freedom, as related in the *Confessio*, would seem to have brought him to the south-east coast, perhaps near Wexford.

The Slemish tradition has, however, been contested, and a place in northern Co. Mayo proposed as the place of Patrick's servitude. The ground for this contestation, which believers in the Slemish tradition have denounced as 'a base attempt to deprive Ulster of its Patrician heritage', is the mention of a 'forest of Foclut' by Patrick in the *Confessio*. After his escape from Ireland, Patrick's divine call to return there came to him as the voice of people who were 'juxta silva

Focluti quae est prope mare occidentale' – beside the forest of Foclut which is near the western sea – crying out to him: 'We beg you, holy youth, that you shall come and shall walk again among us.' Tirechán, himself a native of Mayo, identified the forest of Foclut 'near the western sea' as being in the north of Mayo. If Patrick received a call from people beside the forest of Foclut who called him 'holy youth', these people would have been the ones who had known him during his years of bondage. The partisans of Co. Mayo as the place of Patrick's years of slavery would have his two-hundred-mile route to the port of escape take him to the mouth of the Boyne near Drogheda, a place certainly familiar to Patrick in later years, or to the southern coast of Co. Cork.

The identification of the forest of Foclut with Co. Mayo rests, however, on the writings of the Mayoman Tirechán. Northern Mayo was 'near the western sea', but can we be sure that in writing of the 'western sea' Patrick was not describing it from a British viewpoint and referring to the sea to the west of Britain – that is, the channel separating Britain and Ireland? If that were so, the forest of Foclut could have been near Slemish, perhaps in the Glens of Antrim between Slemish and the eastern coast of Co. Antrim. While Tirechán had it that the forest of Foclut was in northern Mayo, he believed nevertheless that Patrick served Miliucc for six years as a slave on Slemish. There was no conflict in this for Tirechán, for he believed that Patrick had been a slave to more than one master. This is not implied by Patrick himself in the *Confessio*.

Ulster or Connacht? The steep volcanic slopes of Slemish or the more distant forest plain in the neighbourhood of Killala? It is unlikely that we will ever be sure of the exact place of Patrick's captivity. Tantalizing as the question may be, more important is what we know of the conversion that Patrick underwent during those years in bondage. Nothing, surely, can be more poignant in describing this change than Patrick's own words in his *Confessio*.

Suddenly transported from a luxurious life of freedom in a civilized and sophisticated Romanized Britain, to a state of bondage in an alien, comparatively primitive world, Patrick turned for comfort to the God of his Christian family, the God to whom in his carefree youth he had given little thought. Patrick endured trials and hardships, but as he pastured his master's flocks, he tells us, 'I used to pray many times a day. More and more did the love of God and my fear of him and faith increase and my spirit was moved so that in a day [I said] from one up to a hundred prayers, and in the night a like number, besides I used to stay out in the forests and on the mountain and I would wake up before daylight to pray in the snow, in icy coldness, in rain ...' Patrick was sure that this change of heart was due to the fervour of the Holy Spirit burning in him.

There, whether in the western forest or on the northern mountain, Patrick relates that in his sleep he heard a voice telling him that he would soon depart for his homeland. Not long after, he was vouchsafed a prophecy announcing to him that his ship was ready. Muirchú recounts that an Angel, Victoricus, appeared to Patrick to announce the details of his escape. Although Patrick had never been to the harbour where the ship lay, nor knew anyone there, he testified that by God's help he found his way to it, two hundred miles distant from his place of captivity.

When Patrick reached the port (perhaps Drogheda – perhaps Wexford) the ship was ready to set out, but the steersman refused to let him sail with them. Patrick returned, praying the while, to the hut where he had found lodging, but before he reached it, one of the crew had come after him, shouting to him to come back quickly, that he was being called. Patrick had no doubt that it was his prayers which had wrought a change of heart in the crew. They told him. 'Come, ... we are admitting you out of good faith ... make friendship with us in any way you wish.' It seems that the men of the crew expected Patrick to seal a bond of friendship with them by sucking their breasts. This may have been a rite of brotherhood in imitation of the bond of fosterage. For fear of God, he tells us, he rejected such an act, but hoping for their conversion to Christianity, he boarded ship and set out with them.

From whichever port Patrick set out, his sea-journey, he tells us, lasted three days. This length of voyage would have taken him from eastern or south-eastern Ireland to north-western France. Patrick may have sailed from a more southerly port in Ireland than Wexford; certainly he appears to have landed in a western extremity of what was then Gaul, for he tells us in the *Confessio* that after landing, the party wandered in wild uninhabited country for twenty-eight days. Travelling for about eight hours each day, covering about twenty-five miles per day, the men could have walked seven hundred miles in the four weeks that they were on the road, taking them from a possible landing-place on the western coast of Brittany (allowing for meandering, as they did not know the country) well into the heart of Gaul, at least as far as Auxerre, where there is reason to believe that Patrick stayed.

Food ran out during the cross-country journey. Patrick, who, it seems, was able to converse with the crew in some common language, must have told them of the mightiness of God. Fearing death from starvation they taunted him that his 'God' had not come to their aid. Patrick was not taken aback. He called on his interlocutors to have faith, and they would be provided for. A herd of swine appeared fortuitously. The party slew many of them and nourished themselves on the meat. The men thereafter respected Patrick, gave thanks to God, and continued to find victuals along their road. (The famous hounds with which we are often told the party was travelling owe their origin to a reading of the Latin *carne*, meat, as *canes*, dogs, in paragraph 19 of the *Confessio*.)

A further detail related in the *Confessio* remains obscure, as it is not clear at what juncture the incident occurred. 'And a second time, after many years, I was taken captive,' writes Patrick. In the sequence of events he is relating it appears that this may have occurred during the course of his escape-journey with the sailors. However, it appears that it occurred at some time after the twenty-eight-day treck. In the early fifth century, barbarian tribes were pouring across Gaul in the wake of the Vandals, who came in 406. It may well have been a party of such barbarians who held Patrick captive. On the first night of this second captivity. Patrick heard a divine prophecy promising him that it would only last for two months. On the sixtieth day of his captivity, in accordance with the prophetic promise, he was delivered from his captors.

Patrick's sojourn in Gaul has been questioned, but the details of his escape-voyage from Ireland do appear to lead there. They hardly correspond with a disembarkation in western Britain, and the wording of the *Confessio* implies that Patrick did not reach Britain and his family until a few years later – 'et iterum post paucos annos in Britaniis eram'. Patrick's only reference to Gaul, many years later in the *Confessio*, is in paragraph 43, where he expressed his desire to go, not only to Britian to see his homeland and kinsfolk, but 'as far as Gaul to visit the brethren there so that I might see the faces of the holy ones of my Lord ...'. This implies that there were in Gaul priests or monks, probably a community, with whom he was acquainted.

A further indication that Patrick had actually been in Gaul may be found in his *Letter to Coroticus* in which, in the fourteenth paragraph, he wrote of how the practice obtained in Gaul of ransoming back from the pagan Franks the baptized Christians whom they had taken captive. This does imply Patrick's familiarity with Gaul during the period of heathen Frankish occupation. The Franks, a Germanic people, occupied most of Gaul north of the River Loire between 428

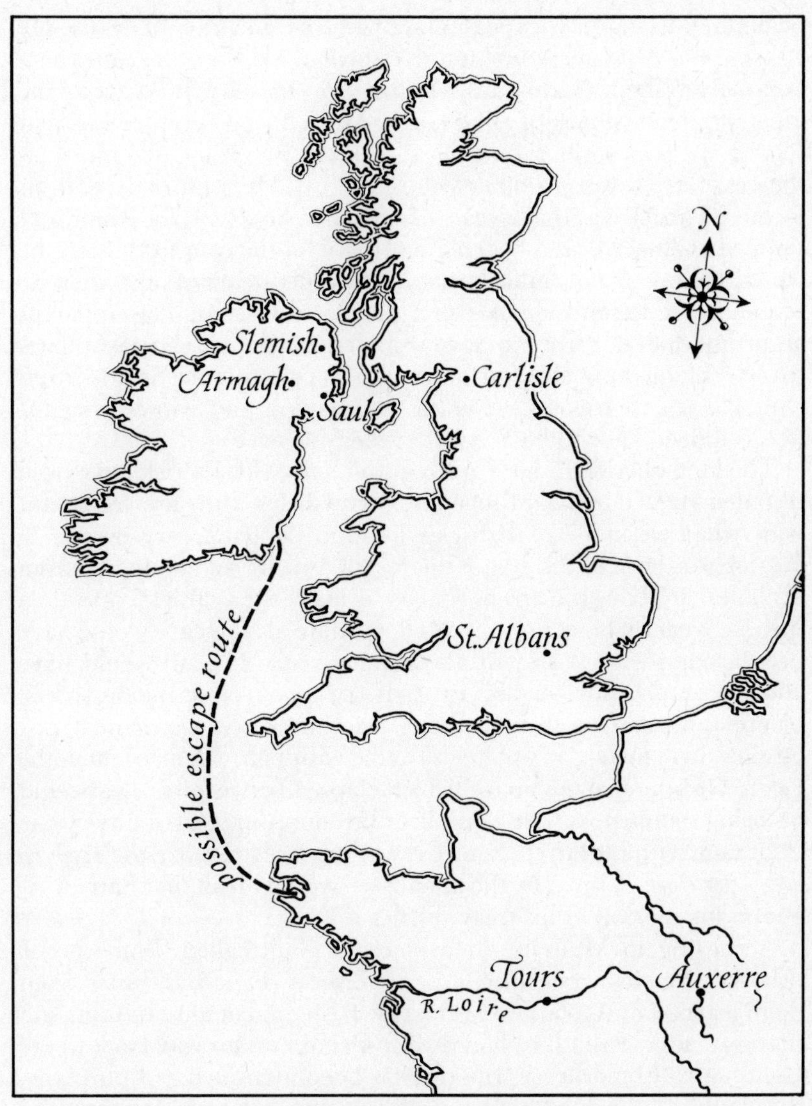

Map of Patrick's early routes

and 480, after which date they accepted Christianity.

Muirchú states unequivocally that Patrick spent some years in Gaul, although according to his account, it appears that this was *after* a sojourn in Britain with his family and when he had reached the age of thirty. 'So he crossed the southern British sea,' writes Muirchú, 'and beginning his journey through Gaul with the intention of eventually crossing the Alps, according to the resolve of his heart, he came on a very holy bishop, Germanus, who ruled in the city of Auxerre, the greatest lord in almost of all of Gaul.' Muirchú goes on to tell us that Patrick spent a considerable time at Auxerre, according to some of his sources, forty years, to others, thirty. If, as Muirchú had been informed, Patrick was thirty years of age when he set out for Rome and stopped at Auxerre, and he remained there for thirty or forty years, he would have been an unlikely sixty or seventy years of age when he responded to the missionary call to return to Ireland. This apparent absurdity does not seem to have troubled Muirchú, who also relates that Germanus appointed an 'older man', a priest named Segitus, to go with Patrick to Ireland, to be his companion and witness. Segitus would indeed have to have been a venerable age.

The long-cherished dates given in the *Annals* for Patrick have been disputed by a number of scholars. Nevertheless they are consonant with what we know of Patrick's life and contemporary events. If Patrick was born at the end of the fourth century and abducted from his home at about the age of sixteen, around the year 415, and then spent six years in bondage in Ireland, the date of his escape would have been around 421. A stay of about eight years in Gaul would have allowed ample time for him to study for and receive minor orders, before returning to Britain about the time of St Germanus' first mission there in 429. It would also agree with Patrick's mention in the *Confessio* of the 'paucos annos' which elapsed between his escape and his being reunited with his kinsfolk in Britain. A sojourn of three years in Britain with his family before returning to evangelize the Irish in 432 – the date claimed by the annalists – would mean that Patrick set out on his mission in his early thirties.

According to Muirchú, at a place in Gaul called 'Ebmoria' or 'Eboria' Patrick met disciples of Bishop Palladius, and from them learned of the failure of the first Irish episcopal visitation, and that its leader, Palladius, had died in Britain on his way back to the Continent. 'Ebmoria' or 'Eboria' has been identified as Eburobica, the name of the modern town of Avrolles between Auxerre and Soissons. Then, according to Muirchú, Patrick went to a saintly bishop named Amathor who consecrated him a bishop. Here again we have chronological problems. The known Bishop St Amathor was the predecessor of Germanus at Auxerre and had died in 418, several years before Palladius was sent to the Irish in 431.

What can we make, then, of these statements? Perhaps little more than that Patrick was at Auxerre at some time, and that he was probably a student under Germanus. If he reached Gaul as early as before 418, rather than around the traditional date of 422, he could have received minor orders from Bishop Amathor. Another suggestion has been made that Patrick was consecrated bishop in the basilica dedicated to St Amathor at Auxerre, and that Muirchú's statement stemmed from his misreading or misunderstanding of an earlier text or tradition that 'he went to St Amathor to be consecrated', which referred to the basilica of St Amathor rather than to the Saint himself.

Patrick's contemporaries in the Christian hierarchy in Gaul were outstanding personalities and scholars of exceptional calibre. Patrick may have had contact with a number of important monasteries, but tradition has long held that he was at Lérins and Auxerre, and possibly at Tours, so that it seems that it must have been the community of one of those places who were the 'brethren' whose faces Patrick tells us years later that he longed to see again. Patrick himself does not mention Lérins (which is just off the south coast of France, opposite Cannes) in either of his writings, nor do we find mention of Lérins in Muirchú's *Life*, but the fragmentary *Dicta Patricii*, which may be genuine at least in part, records his saying: 'I had the fear of God as my guide for my journey through Gaul and Italy and also on the islands in the Tyrrhenian sea.' The island monastery of Lérins was founded by Honoratus, Bishop of Arles; it counted among its early community such contemporaries of Patrick as St Hilary of Arles (401–99) and St Vincent of Lérins, who entered the monastery about 425 and was outstanding for his erudition even among the highly educated men attracted there by its spiritual discipline.

The monastery at Marmoutier near Tours was founded by St Martin, Bishop of Tours (316–97), after he had first established a community of hermits at Ligugé in 371. The great monastic complex at Marmoutier became a leading centre of western Christianity, and its influence which spread through Gaul would certainly have affected Patrick's studies.

The Auxerre monastery was founded by St Germanus (*c.* 378–448). Germanus was described by Muirchú as 'the greatest lord in almost all of Gaul' because he had been appointed provincial governor of the region in Gaul called Armorica by the Roman Emperor Flavius Honorius. It was in 418, when he succeeded St Amathor as Bishop of Auxerre, that he established the monastery which flourished near that city.

While there is no tradition of Patrick's association with the monastery of St Victor at Marseilles, if he studied in Gaul he could not have remained unaware of its importance, and would probably have encountered some of its alumni. That monastery was founded by the Abbot St John Cassian (360–453), a native of Romania, in 415, on the ascetic models of the communities where he had been trained in Palestine and in the Egyptian desert. Cassian espoused the Semi-Pelagian theology that man's moral effort, born of his own initiative, draws grace from God which enables him to strive successfully for salvation. This was in opposition to the doctrine of St Augustine. Patrick's contemporary St Prosper of Aquitaine (*c.* 390–463) lived for many years in the Marseilles monastery.

As mentioned earlier, it was to suppress the Pelagian heresy which persisted in Britain that Pope Celestine I sent Germanus from Auxerre to Britain with Lupus, Bishop of Troyes in 429. Patrick himself could have accompanied that delegation. In 447, Germanus was obliged to return to Britain again on a similar mission, when he was accompanied by Severus, Bishop of Trèves, and a party of eleries.

Patrick would have been cognizant of important councils of the Church convened to debate theological issues. The Council of Ephesus in 431 treated the question of Christ's relation to God the Father and the relationship of the human and the divine in Christ himself. The Council of Orange in 441 under the presidency of St Hilary of Arles dealt more with disciplinary matters, in an effort to maintain unity of practice and suppress deviations.

St Celestine I, Pope from 422 to 432, succeeding Boniface I, was an energetic pontiff who attacked the unorthodox teaching of Nestorius, Patriarch of Constantinople, that Christ's human and divine natures were independent, and he was a vigorous opponent of the Pelagian theology which minimized the importance of divine grace in man's salavation. It was this Pope Celestine I who consecrated Palladius in 431 and sent him as the first bishop to the Irish. The other great Pope of Patrick's time was the eminent St Leo the Great, who reigned from 440 to 461; he made strenuous efforts to preserve orthodoxy and maintain papal supremacy in the Church in Western Europe, as the Roman Empire disintegrated in the West.

Critics of the traditional dates for Patrick's mission have suggested that the annalists chose 432 for his return to Ireland purposely to coincide with the date of Palladius' being sent to Ireland by Pope Celestine I. But is it not probable that the two events occurred about the same time? The Pope's concern for the Christians in Ireland in 431 may well have arisen from reports sent to Rome by Germanus after his mission to Britain in 429. A period commencing about 432 for Patrick's mission in Ireland is also consistent with the period of the reign of the Irish King Loegaire (son of Niall of the Nine Hostages) with whom Patrick had to contend in his missionary exploits, and who died, according to the annalists, about 462–3.

If the exact sequence of events is uncertain, the events themselves are fairly clear. As the author of the notes on *Fiacc's Hymn* from the Franciscan *Liber Hymnorum* says, Patrick possibly came to Britain from Gaul, with Germanus' party to exterminate the Pelagian heresy.

Important as the period of preparation and theological study in Gaul may have been to Patrick's future apostolate, it was the call to return to the Irish that was decisive. Patrick tells us in the *Confessio* that he received this call when he was in Britain, at last reunited with his family. They urged him to remain at home with them, but 'in a vision of the night', Patrick explans, 'I saw a man whose name was Victoricus, coming as if from Ireland with innumerable letters, and he gave me one of them and I read the beginning of the letter, 'The voice of the Irish', and as I was reading ... I seemed at that moment to hear the voice of those who were beside the forest of Foclut which is near the western sea, and they were crying out as if with one voice, "We beg you holy youth, that you shall come and shall walk again among us." And I was stung intensely in my heart ...'

Muirchú gives the same name, Victoricus, to the Angel who comforted Patrick in divine apparitions during his time in slavery, and announced to him the time and the means of his escape to freedom. It seems we may identify this Victoricus with a cleric of that name who had visited Britain from Gaul about the time of Patrick's birth. A disciple of St Martin of Tours, Victoricus became Bishop of Rouen, and his visit to Britain in the last decade of the fourth century was to gain support among the bishops in Britain for the reforms introduced by St Martin. He was a contemporary and co-disciple of St Amathor, Bishop of Auxerre, the predecessor of Germanus in that see, and was remembered as a pioneer in the work of proselytizing the barbarians. It may have been his fame in this capacity which reached Patrick. In popular Patrician legend, Victoricus has became the angel 'Victor'. Pilgrims climbing Skerry will still be shown the rock bearing the Angel Victor's footprint at the spot *p. 34*
where he appeared to Patrick.

III
Patrick the Missionary

Most of what has come down to us of Patrick's missionary experiences and his itineraries and foundations in Ireland is based on the account of Muirchú, written a little over two hundred years after Patrick's death, or on the account of Tirechán, written a decade or so before Muirchú's; or on the richly embroidered stories included by later hagiographers, who combined a scant regard for historicity with a large desire to glorify their subject.

It is essential, therefore, to scrutinize Patrick's own writings to discover what they can reveal of his missionary years in Ireland. The *Confessio*, although autobiographical, names no places or persons, but a careful reading does convey a very real sense of Patrick's struggle, the situation he had to confront, the difficulties he encountered, and the great scope of his activities.

Patrick wrote the *Confessio* in Ireland after he had been there for many years as a missionary. He describes himself as being, at the time of writing, 'in senectute mea', in his old age. He also tells us, in mentioning a sin committed in his youth, that he had confessed that sin before his ordination to the diaconate, at least thirty years previously. Patrick would have had to have been ordained a deacon after the age of twenty-two when he escaped from his captivity as a slave. The most likely time for his ordination to the diaconate would have been between the age of twenty-two and thirty. In any case we can say that he was at least in his mid-fifties when he wrote the *Confessio*, more probably in his sixties, possibly even older. Following the traditional dates with Patrick's birth in the late 390s, his abduction about 415 and escape about 421-2, and the beginning of his mission in Ireland in 432, we must place the date of the writing of the *Confessio* not earlier than around 455.

One of the most important details in the *Confessio* is Patrick's remark that he had baptized several thousand converts (paragraphs 14 and 50). People who had hitherto worshipped idols had come to know God, and the success of their conversion is demonstrated in his statement that sons and daughters of the Irish chiefs had embraced the monastic life as monks and nuns (paragraph 41), and that he had ordained some of the converts to the priesthood (paragraph 50).

Patrick also provides us with glimpses of how he proceeded with his campaign of evangelization, cleverly working within the framework of Irish Celtic society, with its rigid system of values and its own laws. He travelled with a retinue of princelings or young noblemen, the sons of the chieftains, and according to the custom, he paid them for being with him (paragraph 52). He also made payments to the magistrates or judiciars, the men who administered justice in districts he visited (paragraph 53). From time to time, Patrick tells us, he gave presents to the local kings (paragraph 52).

While conforming with the customs which obtained of making gifts and payments, Patrick was careful about accepting gifts. He refused gifts even when to do so caused offence (paragraph 37), and risked offending donors by returning to them the gifts of jewellery which they threw on the altars (paragraph 49).

There were other difficulties in his work. Patrick mentions that he had to endure criticisms and insults (paragraph 37). He suffered the pain and indignity of arrest and imprisonment, was despoiled, and on at least one occasion he was put in irons for fourteen days (paragraph 52). He lived always, he tells us, in fear of death, of betrayal, and of being once again reduced to slavery.

The *Confessio* relates only one particular incident of Patrick's proselytizing activities in Ireland. He tells us he baptized a high-born lady of Irish birth, a very beautiful adult woman. Subsequently she came to him to tell him of an angelic visitation which she had received, calling on her to live a celibate life and to draw closer to God. Within six days of receiving this vocation, the beautiful noblewoman joined other women who were already living as nuns, apparently in a community, many of whom had incurred the wrath of their families and had even been persecuted for choosing that way of life (paragraph 42). By that time, so many single women converts had decided to live a celibate life that Patrick did not know their number, as well as widows and wives who lived chastely.

Throughout his missionary years Patrick was succoured and comforted by the promptings of the Holy Spirit in divine prophecy and visions. At one moment, when he was dishonoured and in despair, he heard divine words of consolation echoing God's words to the Old Testament prophet Zechariah (paragraph 29). Patrick's extraordinary perseverance was rooted in his conviction that God was victorious in him, and that he would therefore be able to overcome all obstacles.

Distressing circumstances prompted the *Confessio*. It was written by Patrick as at once his apology and his testimony, after he had incurred the disapproval of his ecclesiastical superiors. The wording of paragraph 26 of the *Confessio* implies that these clerics came to Ireland and censured him publicly; perhaps there was an episcopal visitation. As a result of their reprehension, Patrick tells us, he fell into disgrace.

The occasion of this disgrace is not entirely clear. In paragraph 32 Patrick writes of a case brought up in Britain against him. We may infer that at the time he was already a bishop, for in paragraph 26 he refers to his superiors' criticism of his arduous episcopate. It appears likely, therefore, that Patrick's ecclesiastical superiors convened in Britain to try him *in absentia* for unorthodox conduct in his Irish mission. Patrick's old and trusted friend and former confessor, who had once told him that he deserved to be raised to the rank of bishop, and had lately told other associates that he would speak up at the trial in Patrick's defence, instead revealed Patrick's youthful sin and publicly discredited him. The meeting at which Patrick's case was heard could well have coincided with the second legation of Germanus to Britain in 447.

Patrick implies that on an earlier occasion, there had been opposition to his elevation to the episcopate. Presumably this would have been many years before, and could have coincided with the date of Germanus' first legation to Britain in 429. There is some doubt from Patrick's wording as to when it was that his old friend discredited him, for he seems to be recalling two separate occasions on which his merits were questioned.

The painful situation for Patrick was that he found his life's work criticized and attacked by his superiors. Moreover, his old and trusted friend and confessor, to whom he had bared his soul, betrayed him and brought him into disgrace.

The nature of the accusations made against Patrick appear to have centred around the question of receiving gifts or rewards, for in paragraph 49 he explains how he returned unsolicited gifts in order to be above criticism, and in paragraph 50, angrily asks whether anyone can say that he has asked even for the price of one shoe in return for ordaining men to the priesthood. Other criticisms levelled against Patrick concerned his lack of education, as he tells us in paragraph 46.

Although Patrick admitted to being cast down by the attitude of his critics, and dismayed by the behaviour of his old friend and confessor, nevertheless he drew strength from his conviction of God's love for him, and of divine approval of his mission to the Irish. Saddened but undaunted he continued his work.

Besides the *Confessio* we have one other primary Patrician source. This is the letter written by Patrick to a British despot, called in the Latin text Coroticus, who had abducted newly-baptized Christians from Ireland and held them captive. In the *Letter to Coroticus* Patrick describes himself as a bishop established in Ireland, and we may conclude that when he wrote the letter he had been in Ireland for twenty years or more, for in paragraph 3 he mentions having already sent one letter with a priest whom he had taught from childhood. A further clue to the date of the *Letter* is in the mention of pagan Franks in paragraph 14. As already mentioned, the Franks, who occupied a large area of Gaul after 428, were converted to Christianity in the last two decades of the century.

A glimpse of Patrick's converts is given in paragraph 3 of the *Letter*, where he writes of the murdered neophytes who were still clothed in the white robes in which they had been confirmed.

While Patrick's own writings tell us nothing of his actual itineraries in Ireland or the site of his foundations there, they do convey most strongly his love for his Irish converts and his concern for them. We remain with a very definite vision of his extraordinary exalted spirituality, and a sense of the relentlessness with which he pursued his apostolate.

IV
Muirchú's Account of Patrick's Mission

Muirchú, the author of one of the two earliest accounts of Patrick's missionary activities in Ireland, was a professional historian. However, two centuries had elapsed between Patrick's death and the time when Muirchú was collecting source-material for his biography of the Saint, so that it is not surprising to find in his work some confusion over names and places, and some details which cannot be reconciled with the *Confessio*. We must also allow for the inclusion of apocryphal material that had accumulated since the Saint's death. Nevertheless, Muirchú's account emerges as that of an educated, sober historian, and we must rely on him for more information about Patrick's mission than Patrick gives us himself.

What were Muirchú's sources? Certainly he would have received information from Aedh, Bishop of Sletty, who died in 699. It was he who commissioned Muirchú to write Patrick's biography, and together they attended the synod convened by Adamnán in 695-7. Muirchú would also have had access to the records of his own father (or spiritual father) Cogitosus, also a professional hagiographer-historian and author of the earliest known biography (written about 650) of Patrick's disciple St Brigid of Kildare. Both Bishop Aedh and Cogitosus could in their youth have conversed with people whose grandparents had lived when Patrick was evangelizing the Irish, so they would have been party to a rich corpus of oral tradition.

As well as enquiring of the older historians and clerics, and sifting the oral tradition, Muirchú was able to work from earlier biographies which have not survived, for he refers to a number of *Vitae Patricii*.

There were also some other manuscript sources from which Muirchú could glean information, works which are mainly of interest to academics; but it is useful, nevertheless, to know a little about them.

One text available to Muirchú was the fifth-century *Hymn of Secundinus* praising Patrick's work and virtues. This is attributed to Sechnall or Secundinus, a fellow-bishop of Patrick's, and was composed in Patrick's lifetime. It is written in the style of that early period made fashionable by Augustine's *Psalm against the Sect of Donatus,* in four-line stanzas, each stanzas beginning with a consecutive letter of the alphabet and in the popular Roman metre called 'versus quadratus', with fifteen syllables per line and a pause after the eighth syllable. The texts of this hymn known to us were all written down after Muirchú's death, but in his lifetime, in the seventh century, the *Hymn* was already a living tradition in both liturgy and popular belief.

Among the documents which may have been available was an earlier letter to Coroticus, mentioned by Patrick in his *Letter to Coroticus* of which we do have a text, and also a letter known to have been written by Patrick to three Irish bishops, Cethiacus, Conall and Sacellus (in Mag Ai, the plain of Co. Roscommon), who were conferring holy orders without consulting him. Again, Muirchú may also have been able to peruse a circular of Patrick, Auxilius and Isernius, issued with Patrick's express authorization about 450, between the date given for the death of Bishop Secundinus, 447, and that given for the death of Bishop Auxilius, 459.

Though Muirchú himself was writing in the seventh century, the earliest texts of his biography available to us are of later date. One in the *Book of Armagh* is dateable to around the year 800, another in two folios was written in the eighth century and is now in the National Library in Vienna, and a third is in an eleventh-century manuscript in Brussels. Unfortunately none of these texts is complete. The earliest complete text, a thirteenth-century manuscript, exhibits considerable signs of reworking. Without pursuing the problems surrounding the establishment of the original text, we shall follow the steps of Patrick as recounted by Muirchú in these, the three earliest available manuscripts.

Muirchú tells us that Patrick arrived in Ireland, his ship laden with religious treasures, at a place in the 'regiones Coolennorum' (this would be the land of the Coolenni or Cualann), at a well-known port called 'Hostium Dee'. The harbour so described, where Patrick and *map, p. 69* his party landed can be identified as Inver Dea, on the estuary of the Vartry River in Co. Wicklow, near Newrathbridge. It is now called the Broad Lough. There, on landing, Patrick decided that he should set out at once for the north to redeem himself legally from his old master in slavery, Miliucc. (If he expected his former master to be still alive, we must surely, in common sense, dismiss the possibility that the missionary Patrick at the time of his return to Ireland was anywhere near sixty years of age, and return to the assumption that he was nearer to thirty.)

Patrick does not attempt a journey overland between the port and Slemish, as when he had escaped years before, but sails along the coast, travelling northwards, stopping first at Inishpatrick, a little grassy island about a mile off the coast, opposite Malahide, a sea-journey of about forty miles which he could have covered between dawn and dark. Thence he continues by boat, passing the coast of Co. Louth, the mouth of Carlingford Lough, and the south-eastern shores of Ulster below the Mountains of Mourne to his left, to sail finally into a sound which Muirchú calls 'Brene'. This must be the strait between Killard Point and Ballyquintin Point, narrows which give entrance to Strangford Lough. Rocks off Killard Point are named St Patrick's Rocks in memory of Patrick's route past them into the sound.

The party lands at the mouth of the Slan and hides the boat there *plate 2* before going a short distance inland to rest. Muirchú's 'Slan' is the Slaney River, once sizeable, now reduced by drainage to a stream. It runs under a little bridge called Fiddler's Bridge on the Strangford-Downpatrick road, not far from the shore of the Lough. The name 'Slan' derives from the Irish word for health, referring to the health-giving properties attached to the Struell Wells area.

A stone with two round holes near the mouth of the Slaney has been identified by Father James O'Laverty (nineteenth-century author of the *History of Down and Connor*) as the spot where, local tradition had it, Patrick first prayed after landing.

Patrick and his party are discovered in their hiding place, according to Muirchú's account, by a swineherd in the service of a man named Dichu. The swineherd, a good-natured man although a pagan, concludes that the strangers are a party of raiders, and he fetches his master to them covertly. It is Dichu's intention to slay the unsuspecting strangers, but as he looks upon Patrick's face, the Lord changes his feelings towards them to benevolence. Patrick preaches the faith to Dichu, who believes then and there, and Patrick remains with him for a few days.

Muirchú tells us that the place where Dichu found Patrick was the site, in his day, of a barn named after Patrick. This place is Saul, Co. Down, whose name derives from the Irish *sabhal* meaning barn. According to tradition, Patrick founded his first church in Ireland in Dichu's barn. On the site now stands a Protestant church, built in 1932 and designed by Henry Seaver of Belfast in a style supposed to be that of an Early Christian church, with a Round Tower. It was

erected to commemorate the fifteen-hundredth anniversary of Patrick's arrival there as a missionary, and to mark the place where he preached to his first convert. The fine window in the church. depicting Patrick and the boat in which he sailed into Strangford Lough, is by the Dublin artist Catherine O'Brien, a pioneer in the An Túr Gloine stained-glass works co-operative. Saul Church attracts visitors from all over the world. Special services are held there on St Patrick's feast day, 17 March, but it is also in regular use as the parish church for the local Church of Ireland community.

The present church at Saul replaced a plain whitewashed church building without tower or spire, built about 1770 on the site of a ruined ancient abbey which had suffered many vicissitudes, from the attacks of Viking marauders to its plundering by the troops of Edward Bruce in 1316. At that time it was an Augustinian Priory, having been restored in the twelfth century by St Malachy for monks of that order.

While the Protestant community commemorated the fifteen-hundredth anniversary of Patrick's landing and the baptism of his first neophyte at Saul by the building of the new church, the Roman Catholic community commemorated the same event by erecting Stations of the Cross and an open-air altar on the slopes of Slieve Patrick, and setting a thirty-two-foot-high statue of Patrick on the summit. There is a claim that the sculptor modelled the Saint's face

on the fine head of the then Protestant Primate of Ireland, Dr D' Arcy, Archbishop of Armagh. Bronze panels around the base of the statue depict scenes from Patrick's life. Annually, on the first Sunday of June, Mass is celebrated on the open-air altar.

Muirchú's narrative goes on to relate how Patrick leaves his boat in the care of his proselyte Dichu and is soon on his way to Slemish, to accomplish his intention of paying the price of his redemption from slavery to his former master, Miliucc, hoping thereby to win Miliucc's esteem and to convert him. Advance scouts seem to have brought Miliucc news of Patrick's coming, before he and his party reach Slemish. The elderly, proud old chieftain, unwilling to be converted to the new faith, and aghast at the prospect of being in some way subject to his former slave, sets fire to himself in his own dwelling, and is burned to death with his possessions.

When Patrick reaches the south side of Slemish (at a spot which was marked in Muirchú's time by a cross) he looks over the place where he had served as a slave and sees, where the chieftain's dwelling had been, his charred funeral pyre. Deeply disconcerted by Miliucc's action. Patrick remains in silent meditation for two, almost three hours. Then, weeping and sighing, he prophesies that none of Milicucc's sons or their descendants will ever succeed him in the kingship of his territory, but will be slaves for ever. After praying and signing himself with the cross, he speedily retraces his steps to Saul and stays for many days at Dichu's residence, going about over the whole plain, which he comes to love, and witnessing the flowering of Christianity in the region.

The countryside around Saul counts several places traditionally associated with Patrick but not specifically named by Muirchú. West of Downpatrick is the place now called Struel Wells where Patrick is reputed to have come from Saul to bathe. A church stood on the site for centuries, but the ruined, rectangular gabled edifice now opposite the 'Drinking Well' in a grassy hollow, dates only from a rebuilding about 1750. The therapeutic qualities of the waters at Struel, attributed to their sanctification by Patrick, have been famed for time out of mind. The 'Drinking Well' is a circular structure of rubble-stone with a domed stone roof. The 'Eye Well', so-named because its waters are reputed to cure diseases of the eye, is a rectangular edifice with a pyramidal roof. Adjacent to these wells are rectangular gabled buildings, the bath-houses, one for men and one for women. The waters run through the two bath-houses and then reunite to join the main stream.

The night of 23 June and the Friday before Lammas are the special occasions for pilgrimage to Struel Wells. Writing in 1837, Samuel Lewis reported the belief that on St John's Eve the water rose in the wells supernaturally, and that the penitents and pilgrims made circuits around the wells, praying, as a cure for 'obstinate and chronic distempers'. A stone on the brow of the hill overlooking the wells, known as St Patrick's Chair or St Patrick's Bed, was also the centre of ritual circuits.

To return to the account of Patrick's missionary activity around Saul: Easter is approaching, and Patrick and his party discuss where they shall celebrate it. Patrick has by that time learned that the most important of the Irish kings, Loegaire, has his stronghold in the Boyne valley at Tara, and he is divinely inspired to go there to drive *p. 24* the first invincible wedge into the heart of idolatry in Ireland.

It is clear that Patrick's strategem was to start at the top, by converting the leading monarch, so that his subjects, the vassals and the lesser kings, should naturally follow him in the new faith.

Patrick and his party bid farewell to Dichu, but do not attempt to travel across the mountains, or around them, to reach the Boyne valley. They launch their boat again and sail out of the Lough and down the coast into the harbour, known to Muirchú as 'Inver Colpthi'. This was the mouth of the Boyne at Drogheda, a journey of about fifty miles. Leaving their boat they travel on foot until, that evening, they reach the place described by Muirchú as the burial place of the men of Fiacc. This, he tells us, had according to legend been dug by the men, or rather the slaves, of the wizard Feccol Fechertni. There Patrick pitches his tent and, with his party, prepares piously for Easter.

The Boyne valley region is renowned for its prehistoric burial places, the mounds of Dowth, Knowth and Newgrange. The necropolis of the men of Fiacc where Patrick camped was on the Hill of Slane, on the northern side of the Boyne about twelve miles from the *plate 3* mouth of the river where he had left his boat. Presumably, Patrick and his followers had followed the northern bank of the river. Had they come along the southern bank, they would have had to cross a dangerous ford at Slane in order to ascend the hill.

The Easter of Patrick's arrival, Muirchú relates, coincided with an important pagan festival. It was celebrated with incantations, feats of magic and idolatrous rites, by wizards, sorcerers, soothsayers and experts in witchcraft, convoked to the court of Loegaire with kings, commanders, governors, princes and leading citizens. Muirchú likens the occasion to the gathering at the Babylonian court of Nebuchadnezzar. One taboo associated with this pagan festival was that no one might light a fire anywhere, that night, before a fire had been kindled in the royal household.

Patrick, on the Hill of Slane, lights his Paschal fire; it is seen across the plain below, and as far as Loegaire's stronghold on the Hill of Tara to the south-west. Loegaire calls his elders and senior advisers and asks them: 'What is this? Who dares to commit this abominable wickedness in my kingdom? Let him be put to death? (In Muirchú's

Latin version: 'Quid est hoc? Quis est qui hoc negas ausus est facere in regno meo? Pereat ille morte.') The elders and senior advisers are unable to name the culprit, but the wizards tell the King with foreboding that if the offending fire is not extinguished that very night, it will never be put out, but will surpass all the fires lit according to their own customs; that the coming kingship of he who lit the fire will overpower them all, and seduce the people, and that all powers shall submit to it, and it shall be all-encompassing and continue for ever and ever.

King Loegaire's chief soothsayers, Lothroch (*alias* Lochru) and Lucetmael (*alias* Ronal), have for two or three years been predicting the coming of an alien doctrine from across the sea. It would be proclaimed by few and accepted by many, and would overthrow kingdoms, suppress the monarchs who resisted it, destroy the local gods, expel the wizards, and reign for ever and ever. The soothsayers have even described the man who will bring the new cult as having a crook-headed staff ('Assiciput' – *asica caput* or adze-head). Leogaire is deeply perturbed by the warnings of his wizards. Determined that the fire on Slane shall not prevail, he decides to put an end to the matter by going there at once to kill those who have perpetrated the sacrilegious act.

Chariots are yoked, twenty-seven in number in accordance with pagan lore, and the King sets out with his wizards Lucetmael and Lochru and the most distinguished members of his court, to confront the offenders. On the way, the wizards advise Loegaire to allow them to have the culprit brought to him to make obeisance, rather than to demean himself by going to meet him. The wizards propose that they shall then debate with the rival in the King's presence so that he can test them. Loegaire acquiesces, and when his party reach the Hill of Slane they dismount from their chariots and horses outside the enclosure where the pascal fire had been lit, and Patrick is summoned to come outside to them. The wizards urge Loegaire and his party not to stand when Patrick arrives, and predict that anyone who does so will become a follower of the new faith.

Patrick comes out to Loegaire's party singing in his heart the words of the psalmist in the Nineteenth Psalm (v.8). One of Loegaire's men, Ercc, not heeding the wizards' warning, rises as Patrick approaches. Patrick blesses him and Ercc becomes a believer.

A discussion ensues, in the course of which the wizard Lochru arrogantly insults the Christian faith. (Muirchú's account presupposes some slight knowledge, at least, of Christianity in pre-Patrician pagan Ireland.) Patrick confidently asks the Lord to punish

Lochru for his blasphemous words. At once Lochru is thrust up in the air and then dashed to the ground, head first, smashing his skull against a stone and dying before the eyes of the assembly of pagans, who are filled with fear.

Loegaire, enraged, orders his men to seize Patrick and kill him. Patrick stands and cries out in a loud voice: 'Let God arise and scatter his enemies, and let those who hate him flee from his sight.' Darkness falls and confusion reigns among the pagans, who attack one another in error. Then an earth-tremor locks their chariots together as they hurtle away, so that most are killed in the melée; only Loegaire, his wife and six others of his party survive. Loegaire's wife comes to Patrick to beseech him not to destroy her husband, promising that the King shall become a worshipper in Patrick's faith. Loegaire comes to Patrick and feigns conversion by genuflecting before him; then planning to kill Patrick he calls him aside, but is foiled. As Patrick and his disciples, eight men and a boy, approach Loegaire, suddenly he is unable to see them; his men can discern only some deer and a fawn in their place. Shaken and humiliated, Loegaire and the survivors of his party return to Tara.

The next day, Easter Sunday, Loegaire and his court discuss the extraordinary events at Slane as they feast in the banqueting hall of the royal fort at Tara; suddenly, although the doors are closed, Patrick and five of his followers appear in their midst. (Muirchú points out to his readers the analogy between this miracle and Christ appearing in a room with closed doors.) Only one of the pagans rises to his feet, the poet Dubthach, and as had happened on the previous day with Ercc, Patrick blesses him and he becomes a believer. A young poet named Fiacc who is staying with Dubthach becomes a neophyte. (He ends his days as the first Bishop of Sletty, the predecessor of that Aedh, Bishop of Sletty, who commissioned Muirchú to write his *Life of Patrick*.)

Patrick accepts the pagans' invitation to join their banquet. In front of the others, Lucetmael pours some liquid from his goblet into Patrick's. Patrick blesses his goblet. All the contents are changed to a substance like ice except the drops that Lucetmael has added. Patrick pours these out and blesses the cup a second time, when the contents return to their first liquid state, to the amazement of the assembly.

Lucetmael then challenges Patrick to perform signs and wonders, the first being to bring down snow on the land. Patrick replies that he refuses to bring about what might be contrary to God's will. Casting magic spells, Lucetmael then brings down a heavy fall of snow on the plain. Then Patrick challenges Lucetmael to remove the snow.

Lucetmael replies that he cannot do so before the next day. 'You can wreak evil but not good,' Patrick tells him. 'Not so with me.' He blesses the surrounding plain, and in an instant the snow vanishes before the eyes of the amazed pagans.

Invoking demons, Lucetmael then brings down darkness. Patrick challenges him to lift it, but he is not able to do so. In prayer, Patrick imparts a blessing. Light returns and the sun shines before the court, who acclaim this feat.

Loegaire then orders both Lucetmael and Patrick to throw their books into the water, promising to venerate the one whose books emerge undamaged from the test. Knowing something of the Christian baptismal rite, and believing that Patrick has a special power over water, Lucetmael refuses this challenge. Loegaire then suggests a test of the books by fire; again Lucetmael protests, saying that Patrick has power over fire as well as water, alternately worshipping both. Patrick denies this; he asks that Lucetmael wearing his, Patrick's, cloak, and one of Patrick's disciples, Benignus, wearing Lucetmael's cloak, shall go into a hut built half of green wood and half of dry wood. The hut is hastily built. Lucetmael goes into the part made of green wood and Benignus into the part made of dry wood. Then, before the assembled crowd, the hut is set on fire. While Patrick prays, the fire consumes Lucetmael and the green wood, leaving only Patrick's cloak untouched. Benignus, on the other hand, emerges unscathed from the dry wood which does not burn, although Lucetmael's cloak which Benignus had been wearing is consumed by the flames.

Loegaire, infuriated by the death of his wizard, rushes at Patrick, and would have slain him, had not God intervened. Then Patrick warns Loegaire that unless he believes he will soon die, struck down by the wrath of God as have been many of his people. Loegaire, by now terrified, assembles his elders and advisors and tells them that it is better for him to believe than to die. With their consent, he accepts conversion that same day, as do many others. Patrick leaves Loegaire with a prophecy that although he himself would live on to reign, because he has opposed him and tried to impede his mission, none of his descendants will ever succeed him.

Then, setting out from Tara, Patrick pursues his mission; his preaching is confirmed by miraculous signs.

Patrick is next back in Ulidia, in confrontation with an evil and malevolent tyrant named Macuil, whose rugged hilltop stronghold is a place called Druimm Moccu-echach (in what is now the barony of Iveagh). It was Macuil's savage custom to seize and murder passing travellers. One day, Macuil espies Patrick walking calmly and peaceably near his stronghold and decides to kill him brutally as he has killed others; gathering his henchmen, he points out Patrick as the trickster who has deceived and misled many, and enjoins them to accompany him to test the power of Patrick's God.

This they hope to do by the ruse of bringing to Patrick one of their number who feigns to be gravely ill. They indicate the supposedly sick man (who lies covered with a blanket) to Patrick and his disciples, and ask for prayers to heal him, hoping that the Christians will fall into the trap and be revealed as charlatans. Patrick perceives their wiles, and tells them boldly: 'It is not surprising that he fell ill.' The heathens then uncover their companion who had pretended to be ill, only now to find him dead. This miracle astonishes Macuil's party, who realize that Patrick is truly a man of God and that they should not have put him to the test. The tyrant regrets what he has done, and submits himself to Patrick's will, surrendering to the God he proclaims. In that hour, Macuil believes, confesses his sins and is baptized. He asks Patrick what punishment he merits for having intended to murder him. Patrick tells Macuil that not he, but God, will judge him. He instructs Macuil to set out for the sea-shore, poorly clad, unarmed, taking none of his belongings, and fasting; at the coast, Macuil is to shackle his own ankles with fetters, throw away the key, and clamber into a small coracle with neither rudder nor oar. He must allow the wind to take him where it will, until he reaches the land where he is to live in exile and obey the commandments of God. Before Macuil leaves, Patrick restores to life the man who having pretended illness, was struck dead.

Macuil reaches the south coast where he fetters himself like a slave, as he had been told to do, throws the key into the sea, and puts out in a boat which is driven by a north wind to the Isle of Man. There he finds the two first Christian missionaries to that place, the bishops Conindri and Rumili; he lives under their rule until eventually he succeeds them in the episcopate.

The next happening finds Patrick resting one Sabbath by the sea, 'near the saltmarsh which is on the northern side not far from the Ox's Neck'. There, Patrick hears some pagan workmen building a rath. When he calls them over and tells them not to work on the Sabbath, they laugh in his face. Patrick tells them that however hard they work, it will be to no avail. And so it happens: a storm blows up in the night and their fortification is washed away.

Patrick, in Armagh, asks a wealthy landowner named Daire for a piece of land for a foundation; he requests a plot of high ground, the

Willow Ridge, 'Dorsum Salicis'. Daire refuses Patrick that land, but gives him a site on lower ground. (Muirchú tells us that in his time this was the Martyrs' burial-place near Armagh). Patrick and his disciples live on that site until one day Daire sends a remarkable horse of his to graze in their meadow. This intrusion vexes Patrick, but Daire's groom ignores his complaint and leaves the horse there – only to find it dead when he returns the next morning. When the groom reports to Daire that Patrick has killed the horse, his irate master orders him to slay Patrick. While the groom is on his way to do this, Daire himself is struck dead. Daire's wife, fearing the power of the Christian missionary, dispatches two men to call the groom back and obtain Patrick's blessing so that they will all be saved. The two emissaries tell Patrick only that Daire is ill, and ask Patrick to send something to cure him. Patrick, knowing what has really occurred, blesses water and tells him to sprinkle some on the horse and take the rest with them. The horse is brought back to life, as is Daire, when the water is sprinkled over him.

Then Daire comes to honour Patrick, bringing as a gift an imported bronze bowl. Patrick merely says '*Grazacham*', which annoys Daire so much that he decides to send his men to take the huge bowl back. When they tell Patrick that they have come to recover the gift, he says only '*Grazacham,* take it.' The men come back to Daire and report what has happened, at which Daire exclaims: '*Grazacham* when you give it, *grazacham* when you take it away – he shall have his bowl.' And he takes it back to Patrick himself, and congratulates him on his firmness, and gives him also the ridge he had originally asked for (the site, Muirchú tells us, of the city of Armagh). Together, Patrick and Daire climb up to the site to admire it. There they find a hind with her fawn (at the spot where, in Muirchú's time, the altar of one of the Armagh churches had been placed). Patrick prevents his followers from killing the fawn, which he carries about on his shoulders. The hind becomes as docile as a ewe and follows them, until Patrick frees the fawn in a place to the north of Armagh.

The next episode takes place back in 'Inis'. A tough, miserly and greedy man has forcibly driven away from the pasture where they were grazing the two oxen which draw Patrick's cart. Patrick lays a curse on the field, that it will never be of use to the man or to his heirs. The sea comes up and the meadow becomes a saltmarsh, to remain forever infertile.

Muirchú concludes his *Life* by recounting what he calls 'a few of Patrick's numerous miracles', but he does not state where any of these events took place. A British princess, Monesan, moved by the Holy

Spirit, is filled with an ardent desire to know and serve the one true God. For that reason, she is reluctant to marry, despite her parents' insistence; they beat and drench their daughter, but she continues adamant in her refusal to marry, and urgently enquires about God. (It would seem that the family must have been lapsed Christians, following the barbarian invasions in Britain, or heathens of Christian extraction.) The parents have heard of Patrick and his nearness to God, and decide to go to Ireland with their daughter to find him in the hope that he will enlighten her. After long search they find him. Patrick hears Monesan's declaration of belief in God and baptizes her with water and with the Holy Spirit, upon which she falls prostrate to the ground and delivers up her spirit. (Muirchú tells us that in his day, her relics were venerated in a nearby cell, to which they had been removed twenty years after her death and burial, but he does not name the place.)

A second miracle recounted occurs when, in the darkness, Patrick on his way to pray sees heavenly signs, and asks his beloved saintly young disciple Benignus whether he, too, perceives them. Benignus declares that he sees a divine vision – the Son of God and his angels, revealed by the heavens opening; Patrick tells Benignus that by this he knows he shall be his worthy successor. The two go on to their usual place of prayer, where they kneel in the river. When Benignus says that he can no longer endure the cold of the water, Patrick tells him to step down from the place where he is to a lower position; but there Benignus finds the water so hot that it soon becomes unbearable and he has to clamber on to the bank.

The third and last miracle recounted concerns Coroticus, the British chieftain to whom Patrick's *Letter* was addressed. Patrick writes to the tyrant (apparently a lapsed or apostate Christian) to urge him to cease persecuting and slaying Christians, and to return to the way of truth. It is reported to Patrick that Coroticus has scoffed at his letter, whereupon he prays to God to cast the traitor out from this world and the next. Shortly after this, at a musical performance, Coroticus hears a bard sing that he will soon leave his throne. Before his friends and the assembled courtiers, Coroticus takes on the shape of a little fox, and so makes off, never to be seen again.

On this fairy-tale note, we pass to the account of Muirchú's contemporary Tirechán, whose motive was not merely to glorify the Saint, but to establish his connection with a string of monastic foundations scattered throughout the country.

V
Tirechán's Account of Patrick's Missionary Journeys

Tirechán, the author of the other surviving early account of Patrick's life, was as has been mentioned a contemporary of Muirchú. He was a disciple of Ultán, Bishop of Ardbraccan, Co. Meath, to whose texts Tirechán had access, and from whom he obtained both written and oral tradition concerning Patrick. Like Bishop Aedh of Sletty, Bishop Ultán, who died about 657, could have spoken with men whose grandparents were born in Patrick's lifetime. Tirechán appears to have written his memoir about 670, if we may interpret his mention of 'recent mortalities' as a reference to the plague of 664.

Tirechán's account must be approached with more critical caution than Muirchú's because, written for readers mainly in Meath and Connacht, it was concerned with establishing the extent of Patrick's foundations, and defining the *paruchia Patricii* and the rights attached to it, a matter which had become a cause of dissension by the second half of the seventh century. This motive accounts for what may seem to be 'topomania' on Tirechán's part, in his account of Patrick's doings.

If we must read Tirechán more critically than Muirchú, we still should not relegate his account to the category of the later purely legendary material, and we should remember that most of what he wrote confirmed seventh-century traditions of Patrick's itinerary and exploits. Moreover, it furnished the basis for much of what has been handed down to become hallowed Patrician lore.

In Tirechán's account as in Muirchú's, Patrick arrives as a missionary on the eastern coast of Ireland. He stops at Inishpatrick and founds a church on the mainland, which must be near Holmpatrick, and then goes on again by sea to the mouth of the River Delvin at Gormanstown. Thence he travels into Meath, founding churches at several places, among which Platten, Donaghmore and Donacarny can be identified. At the Slane necropolis he ordains the bishop Kannanus (Ciannán).

map, p. 69

Following the meeting with Loegaire at Tara, Patrick goes to Teltown (Tailteann), the important place of assembly where archaeological finds have confirmed literary accounts of pagan ceremonial festivals; the great festival of Lughnasa – Aonach Tailteann – took place there annually at the beginning of August.

From Meath (where the place named Donaghpatrick in Upper Kells barony commemorates a Patrician foundation), Patrick follows the Blackwater River westwards, founding churches at Derrypatrick, Ratroath and Assey on his way. His route then turns south to Uisneach, another important Celtic assembly site, anciently believed to be the centre of Ireland. Here the Bealtaine festival was held on the first of May. The neighbourhood is rich in ring-forts, cairns and enclosures of the Celtic era. From Uisneach, Patrick turns northwards through Corkaree barony. Co. Westmeath, to cross the River Inny into Co. Longford, where he ordains the bishop Mel, founds a church, and also ordains Gosacht (Gosactus), a son of that Miliucc whom Patrick had served as a slave for seven years. (Tirechán offers no explanation here for the rather surprising introduction of Miliucc's son among Patrick's disciples, but the possible circumstances of his conversion are discussed later in this chapter.)

Patrick's route then goes through Granard, Co. Longford, and over the plain called 'Mag Slecht' that extends from the region of Ballymagauran in Co. Cavan into Co. Leitrim, crossing the Shannon by the ford called '*Snám dá Én*', or 'Swim Two Birds', the delightful ancient name of the stretch of the river between Clonmacnois and Clonburren, Co. Roscommon. At a place named 'Duma Graid' Patrick ordains Ailbe to the priesthood. 'Duma Graid' appears to correspond with the place-name Doogary, found rather frequently in Connacht, there being six townlands of the name in Co. Mayo and two in Co. Roscommon. Presumably the one referred to by Tirechán is the Doogary in Ballintober South barony, Co. Roscommon, a few miles to the north of the place where Patrick forded the Shannon.

At Doogary Patrick tells Ailbe of a beautiful stone altar on the mountain of the descendants of Ailill (from which, it seems, we may infer an earlier Christian presence in the area, and some acquaintance with the neighbourhood on Patrick's part).

Patrick's route continues northwards along the west bank of the Shannon to Moyglas in the barony of Ballintober North, where he makes another foundation which is left in the care of his monks Conleng and Ercleng. Still in eastern Co. Roscommon, Patrick receives from the converted wizard Hono (Ono mac Oengusa) the gift of his dwelling at Elphin. He leaves there in charge the bishop Assicus who is his goldsmith, with his nephew the bishop Betheus, and Betheus' mother, Cipia.

From Elphin, Patrick returns to Doogary and then travels out of that tribal region, north-westwards to Tawney in the barony of Tirerrill, Co. Sligo. There, accompanied by the nun Mathona, a sister of Benignus, he founds a church which is left in the care of a bishop named Cairellus.

From Tawney, Patrick turns southwards, retracing his route past Elphin to Rathcroghan near Tulsk. At the well of Clebach beside Cruachan – probably a well today called Tobercroghoor – he pauses. Rathcroghan, the 'rath of Cruachan', is an ancient Celtic royal burial place, rich in earthworks and earlier megalithic remains. The seven-foot-high standing stone in the middle of a ring-fort is said to mark the burial place of the pagan monarch Daithi. While Patrick and his clerics are assembled at the well, two royal maidens, fair Ethne and red-haired Fedelma, come to wash their hands. These two daughters of Loegaire are being brought up in Connacht by two wizards, the brothers Mael and Caplait. Surprised at the strange appearance of the monks and priests, the girls ask them who they are, and where they come from, to which Patrick replies that it were better for them to believe in the true God than to ask such questions.

'What is God? Where is God? And of whom is God? And where is God's dwelling-place?' the elder of the two girls asks. 'Does your God have sons and daughters? Has he gold and silver? Is he immortal? Is he beautiful? Have many people fostered his son? Are his daughters beautiful and beloved of men? Is he in Heaven or on Earth? On the plain? In what manner does he come to us? In the rivers? In what manner is he come upon? In the mountains? In the glens? Is he young or old? Tell us of him, in what manner is he seen?'

Filled with the Holy Spirit, Patrick answers them: 'Our God is the God of all men, the God of Heaven and Earth, of seas and rivers, of Sun and Moon and stars, of high mountains and deep valleys, the God over Heaven and in Heaven and beneath Heaven. He has his dwelling-place in Heaven and on Earth, and in the sea and in all that is therein. He informs all things, he brings life to all things, he surpasses all things, he sustains all things. He gives light to the Sun and the Moon by night. He makes fountains in the dry land and islands in the seas, and he sets the stars in their places. He has a Son, co-eternal with himself and in his own likeness. Neither is the son younger than the Father, nor the Father older than the Son. And the Holy Spirit breathes in them. The Father and the Son and the Holy Spirit cannot be divided. In truth, I wish to unite you to the

Heavenly King, you who hitherto are daughters of an earthly king. Believe.'

As if with one voice and one heart, the two girls answer: 'In what manner can we believe in the Heavenly King? Instruct us most diligently so that we may see him face to face, inform us and whatsoever you tell us we will do.' Patrick then asks them if they believe that in baptism the sin of their mother and father will be cast off, to which they reply 'We believe.' Patrick asks them if they believe in repentance after sin, in life after death, in resurrection on the Day of Judgment, in the uniformity of the Church. To all of these questions the girls reply 'We believe.' They are then baptized, Patrick blesses the white veils over their heads, and they beg to see the face of Christ. Patrick tells them that unless they receive the sacrament and taste death, they cannot not see Christ's face – to which they reply: 'Give us the sacrament so that we may see the Son, our Bridegroom.' They receive the Holy Eucharist and fall asleep in death. They are wrapped together in one shroud, and are greatly bewailed by their friends. The wizard Caplait, the foster-father of one of the girls, comes to Patrick lamenting. Patrick preaches to him and he, too, believes, and is tonsured. The other wizard, Caplait's brother Mael, comes to Patrick to tell him that he will bring his brother back to his pagan creed, but Patrick preaches to Mael also, and he, too, is converted, and tonsured.

The period of mourning then being over, the bodies of Ethne and Fedelma are buried near the well of Clebach. A circular ditch is dug around the burial place, as is customary (Tirechán adds) among the inhabitants of Ireland.

Patrick founds a church named Shandonagh at 'Ard Licce' (perhaps identifiable with Ardleckna, a townland in the parish of Aughrim, in the same barony as Rathcroghan where the pagan princesses and their tutors had been converted). Patrick's disciple Colman, a monk with deacon's orders, is left in that place.

1 Here on the hill near Slemish in Co. Antrim, according to all the earliest traditions, the slave-lad Patrick drew closer to God in prayer while watching his master's flock, and here he received a heavenly message announcing his way of escape

Overleaf: 2 Returning to Ireland with companions to begin his missionary apostolate to the Irish, Patrick brought their boat into Strangford Lough, to the mouth of the Slaney River in Co. Down, along whose banks they found a suitable landing-place

3 The ruins of 16th-century Franciscan friary, on the site of the earlier Hermitage of St Erc, now crown the Hill of Slane where Patrick lit the first Pascal fire to celebrate Easter in Ireland

4 Mosaics above the nave of the Roman Catholic Cathedral at Armagh show Patrick baptizing the Irish

5 Patrick's boat comes down the River Boyne as far as Trim on his first missionary journey into Meath to convert the great monarch Loegaire of Tara

6 Although Patrick is credited with travels through many parts of Ireland, and with the ascent of many summits, no place is more closely associated with the Saint today than Croaghpatrick, 'the Reek', in Co. Mayo. Here, its rugged slopes are seen from the shore of Clew Bay near Murrisk. From this viewpoint the mountain appears to be a great ridge capped by a dome, while seen from the east or west, it stands out as an exquisitely shaped cone

7 Some relics of St Patrick were preserved in the Augustinian friary at Murrisk, founded by Papal mandate in 1456 on lands donated by the chieftain Thady O'Malley, and this was the starting-place of pilgrimages to Croaghpatrick. The friars were driven out in 1578, but the ruins of the monastery remain, picturesquely situated in the shadow of Croaghpatrick and overlooking the long stretch of Atlantic waters which form Clew Bay, one of the most beautiful inlets of the entire coast of Ireland

At Ard Senlis, Patrick leaves a woman disciple, Laloca (Lallócc); and in the northern part of Ballintober South barony, Patrick consecrates another site.

Patrick goes with a bishop named Cethiacus to his country. Then he passes on to Fuerty in Co. Roscommon, a few miles farther south in Athlone barony near the present border of Co. Galway, and in the tribal territory of the Ui Maine. Patrick places the deacon Justus in charge of that new foundation, leaving with him 'baptismal books' (apparently books of rituals); Patrick's Frankish followers separate from his party there. They are fifteen brothers (two of whom are named as the princes Bernicius and Hernicius) and a sister, Nitria. (Are we then to infer that these Franks had come with Patrick's missionary expedition to Ireland, or that they had joined his force later? Tirechán offers no explanation for their presence.) The Franks continue to evangelize with success, founding a church at Baslick (a place-name which derives from 'basilica') in the barony of Castlerea, Co. Roscommon, on a site Patrick indicated to them when they came to him at Oran in Ballymoe barony where he was at the foundation of Bishop Cethiacus.

Just south of Tulsk in the same county, at a place called 'Duma Selce', Patrick blesses the Ui Briain and stays for some time. Above a lake also called 'Selce', Patrick founds another church and baptizes the Ui Briain.

Immediately afterwards Patrick goes farther west, beside Lough Gara on the border of Co. Mayo, Co. Sligo and Co. Roscommon, and founds another church and digs a well that never runs dry. Still in the neighbourhood of Lough Gara, in Coolavin barony, Co. Sligo, Patrick's next church is established at Killaraght, named for his woman disciple the nun Atrachta, daughter of Talan; there he leaves a paten and chalice.

After an unhappy encounter with the sons of Ercc who steal his horses, for which their descendants are cursed, Patrick reaches the plain called 'Mag Airthig' (this seems to have been to the west of Lough Gara in Costello barony, Co. Mayo). He stops at Tullaghanrock, a townland in Kilcolman parish, and from there travels to 'Drummut Cerrigi' (most probably the Drummad in Frenchpark barony, Co. Roscommon, to the south of Lough Gara). There Patrick comes upon two blood-brothers fighting over the succession

8 Patrick blessed the River Drowes, Co. Leitrim, with an abundance of fish because of the kindness to him of boys who were fishing there

to their father's estates. He intervenes and miraculously halts their duel; telling them to be seated, he makes peace between them. For the sake of their father's soul, they give the land to Patrick, and on it he founds a church. He founds another, a few miles farther west, near the border of Clanmorris and Costello baronies in Co. Mayo, where he preaches and teaches for a week.

The next ecclesiastical foundation is at Mucno's Well, where in Tirechán's time a cross still marked the place where Secundinus (Sechnall) had stood under a leafy elm. From this site, which has not been identified, Patrick goes westwards towards Connemara, to Kilmaine barony in Co. Mayo, where (Tirechán informs us) he builds rectangular churches. (From this we may infer that the usual Patrician foundation was the beehive-type building and that a rectangular edifice was unusual.)

Continuing his journey north-westwards, Patrick stops in the barony of Carra, Co. Mayo, founds a church and baptizes many people. Travelling still north-west, he comes to Aghagower in the barony of Murrisk, where Senachus (Senach) is ordained and made a bishop, and a church is established. The ruined church, oratory and Round Tower at Aghagower probably stand on the site of Patrick's earlier foundation.

At last Patrick comes to the mountain with which he has now been
plate 6 long associated: Croaghpatrick, the peak in the north of Murrisk barony, overlooking Clew Bay with its many islets, and commanding from its summit, 2,500 feet above sea level, a view which extends to the Twelve Pins of Connemara, to the mountains of Achill, to Nephin, and beyond Slieve League to Donegal. On Croaghpatrick Patrick fasts like Moses, Elijah and Christ, for forty days and forty nights. Totmael, Patrick's charioteer, dies and is buried there.

After his penitential forty days on Croaghpatrick, Patrick comes down to establish many churches in the baronies of Murrisk and Burrishoole.

At this point Patrick resurrects from his grave a swineherd who had been slain by soldiers a century before. The man is baptized, makes his confession and is placed back in his tomb.

We next find Patrick among the people of Ui Maine, then founding churches in the 'forest of Foclut', at Faragh near Killala Bay;
plate 7 then at Murrisk, where now the picturesque ruins of a medieval Augustinian friary stand near the shore; then journeying eastwards, through Tawney, Co. Sligo, once again to Aghanagh, also in Tirerill barony; then to a place named Shanco. For the second time Patrick
plate 8 reaches Drumlease, Co. Leitrim. On reaching the River Drowes, he

blesses it to have an abundance of fish, and then goes northwards, into the south of Co. Donegal to a plain called 'Mag Sereth' in Tirhugh barony, passing between Assaroe and the sea. There he founds a church, encamps, and establishes more churches. Four and a half miles off this coast is the small island of Inishmurray, now uninhabited but rich in antiquities, the most impressive of which is a ruined fort converted into a monastery in the sixth century, probably by St Molaise.

Patrick proceeds northwards on his mission to Inishowen, the peninsula in Donegal which is the northernmost part of Ireland, where also pagan and Early Christian monuments have survived. From Inishowen he goes into Co. Tyrone, where he ordains MacErc, Bishop at Ardstraw, then crosses the River Bann to bless a site for a church at Coleraine, Co. Derry, and founds other churches in that region. Patrick next makes his way across the River Bush to Dunseverick on the treacherous northern coast of Co. Antrim (where the crag on which he sat was still known in Tirechán's time as Patrick's Rock). This coast is famous in the ancient pagan legends of Ireland; here was the landing-place of Deirdre and the sons of Uisneach, and off the coast, in the Waters of Moyle, the Children of Lir were turned into swans. In northern Antrim Patrick ordains Bishop Olcanus (Olcán), a disciple whom he had brought up from childhood, and leaves with him relics of the apostles Peter and Paul. Continuing, Patrick founds many churches in what is now the diocese of Connor.

The narrative brings Patrick to Slemish where, during his seven years of slavery, he had looked after Gosacht, the son of Miliucc, and two of Miliucc's daughters, instructing them secretly under oath for fear of the wizards. Surely, in these children of Miliucc who had learned of Christ from the young slave Patrick, we must identify the people who in Patrick's vision called him 'holy youth', and asked him to return to those who had known him as a slave? This Gosacht is the disciple who was ordained by Patrick in Co. Longford. Are we then to assume that Gosacht had managed to adhere to the Christian faith until Patrick's return to Ireland, and then became one of his followers? If so, what are we to make of Muirchú's account of Miliucc's suicide, and Patrick's prophecy that his descendants would all become slaves?

plate 1

Leaving Slemish, and the spot where he had once seen the Angel who had told him that the ship was ready in which he was to escape, Patrick passes into the territory of the Ui Tuirtri. He baptizes many of them; and then, in the barony of Cremorne, Co. Monaghan, he ordains one Victoricus, and founds a great church.

After this circuit, Patrick founds a church for the priest Justanus, attached to the community of Ardbraccan, Co. Meath, and then journeys into Leinster to 'Drummurraghill'. He crosses the plain of the Liffey, where he establishes a church, and he ordains Auxilius and two others, Eserninus and Mactaleus, at Kilcullen, Co. Kildare. The present rambling village of Kilcullen lies about two miles distant from the remains of a medieval walled town built over an earlier settlement with a ruined Round Tower and shafts of ninth-century crosses. At Sletty Patrick ordains Feccus the Fair (Fiacc) and baptizes the children of Dunlaing. Continuing south-westwards through the Gowran Pass to Kells in Co. Kilkenny, he founds a church there, probably on the site of the ruins of the great medieval priory on the edge of the village, and proceeds into Munster, where he baptizes the sons of Natfraich on the Rock at Cashel.

plate 10

Additions by Tirechán to his account in the *Book of Armagh* tell us of a native Irishman, Iserninus, sent from Gaul to Ireland as a missionary at the same time as Patrick. Contrary winds bring Iserninus to a landing place in the south of Ireland, whence he reaches his native territory. There he converts at least one of his own family, preaches, baptizes and founds churches, but his success incurs the wrath of the potentate Endae Cennsalach, who obliges Iserninus and some of his neophytes to flee into exile.

In due course Patrick reaches the potentate's stronghold at Rathvilly (the Fort of the Trees) in Co. Carlow. This impressive royal fort site may still be seen, its summit commanding a view from Lugnaquilla on the north-east to Mount Leinster on the south, and as far as Slievenamon to the south-west and the Slieve Bloom range. At Rathvilly Patrick converts Crimthann, the son of Endae Cennsalach, and obtains from him not only the freedom of the exiled Iserninus and his followers, but also lands in Leinster. Patrick gives the lands to Iserninus, who in turn gives them to his faithful neophytes, with whom he establishes a religious community at Aghade in the barony of Forth, Co. Carlow. There was a convent of Arroasian nuns at Aghade, established there by Dermot, King of Leinster, about 1151, probably on the site of the Early Christian foundation.

While Muirchú says nothing of Patrick's death or burial, Tirechán relates that Patrick lived, like Moses, to the age of one hundred and twenty, and that he was buried at Saul in Co. Down where he had founded his first church in Ireland.

Map of the principal places associated with Patrick's missionary itineraries

VI
The Growth of the Legend

The *Bethu Phátraic*, more widely known as the *Tripartite Life*, is an account of Patrick's life and works written in Irish about 895-901. From internal evidence scholars incline to believe that its compilers reproduced or followed an earlier work of the eighth century, now lost. The *Tripartite Life* contains the foundation of much of what became established Patrician lore, since hallowed by centuries of belief, but we cannot doubt that most of its stories are apocryphal. Only a small part of the *Tripartite* text can be substantiated by the *Confessio* or the *Letter to Coroticus*, or the earlier accounts written by Muirchú and Tirechán which we have followed in the two preceding chapters. While those accounts record a number of extraordinary and miraculous events, not the least of which must be the resurrection, baptism, confession and re-burial of the long-dead swineherd, the *Tripartite Life* is far richer in strange and wonderful deeds of the Saint.

It is in the *Tripartite Life* that we first find the persistent claim that Patrick's place of origin was Dumbarton in Scotland, and also that his mother was named Concessa, a Frankish kinswoman of St Martin of Tours (which is most unlikely as St Martin was born in Hungary). Then, not content with the real marvel of Patrick's conversion and his power to pursue his mission, the *Tripartite Life* tells of miracles accompanying Patrick's birth, and attributes miraculous powers to him even in his childhood, in the manner of the apocryphal 'Gospel of St Thomas' which recounts the childhood miracles of Jesus.

According to the *Tripartite* account the infant Patrick is baptized by a blind cleric named Gornias. Finding no water for the ceremony, Gornias makes the sign of the cross with the infant's hand and instantly a well springs up on the spot. Gornias washes his face in its water, and is not only miraculously cured of his blindness, but is able to read the order of baptism although he had never learned to read.

The *Tripartite Life* assures its readers that Patrick was endowed with grace from his infancy, and was always able to follow the way of truth – this despite Patrick's own admission of youthful sin in his *Confessio*. The *Tripartite* has Patrick, a mere baby in the house of his foster-mother, saving the house from a flood and miraculously igniting a fire by turning drops of water into sparks. As a boy playing with his foster-brothers, he brings home an icicle, breathes on it, and it bursts into flame like tinder. On another occasion he heals his sister Lupait when she falls and wounds her head on a stone.

When Patrick is blamed by his foster-mother for the loss of a sheep he was herding, carried off by a wolf, the wolf comes to the house bringing the sheep, unharmed, in its jaws. On another occasion when a cow goes berserk in the byre and kills five others, Patrick raises the dead cattle to life and cures the mad beast. Following this miraculous feat, when Patrick's foster-father dies the boy embraces the corpse and raises him from the dead.

Patrick turns water into honey which heals all diseases. When he and his foster-mother are ordered to clean the hearth of the monarch's stronghold at Dumbarton, an Angel appears and accomplishes the task for him. The same monarch demands a tribute of butter and curds from Patrick's foster-mother; the lad turns snow into the victuals, but when they are presented to the ruler they return to snow.

The *Tripartite* account of Patrick's abduction has him snatched, not by raiders from Ireland, but by a party of British on their way to ravage 'Armorica' (Brittany). Patrick's parents are slain by the raiders, and he is taken away by them with his two sisters, Lupait and Tigris. The raiding party puts to sea, but for some reason instead of heading directly south to their destination in Brittany, they sail northwards around the coast of Ireland. There they land and sell Patrick to Miliuc (Miliucc), the king of Dalaradia, and his sisters to another master. Patrick serves Miliuc on Slemish as a swineherd for seven years, enjoying frequent consolatory apparitions of the Angel Victor. He instructs Miliuc's son and two daughters in Christian precepts, which they accept. The son is the future Bishop Guasactus of Granard, Co. Longford, whom we meet later in the text in the course of Patrick's mission, and the daughters are the two Emers who will be buried at Clonbroney, Co. Longford.

The account of Patrick's escape from bondage tallies generally with the earlier accounts, save that the *Tripartite* asserts specifically that the boat in which Patrick flees takes him to Britain. Later, spurred on by further visions to accomplish his missionary vocation, Patrick crosses to the Continent where, on his way to Italy, he meets St Germanus. Patrick, aged thirty, decides to stay with Germanus' community at Auxerre. Subsequently he makes his way to Tours to be tonsured in the monastery founded by St Martin. Patrick remains on the Continent for thirty years, during which time he studies also on the island called 'Aralensis', which has been identified as the island monastery of Lérins.

And it is in Gaul, according to the *Tripartite Life*, that Patrick is visited by the Angel Victor, who commands him to proceed to Ireland to bring the pagan Irish into the Gospel net.

With a party of nine Patrick puts out to sea. From what follows, we must conclude that they sailed from a port on the Mediterranean coast of France, presumably intending to travel westwards through the Strait of Gibraltar, around the Iberian peninsula and across the Bay of Biscay to the south of Ireland, but that their boat travelled eastwards through the Mediterranean towards the Holy Land instead. The party first reach an island where Patrick encounters a couple who had in their lifetime known Christ when he dwelt among men, and who had been blessed by the Saviour himself. Although the man and wife must then have been about four hundred years old, they have retained their youthful appearance, while their children and grandchildren exhibit all the normal physical signs of extreme old age. The ever-young-looking husband tells Patrick that he had been warned prophetically of his arrival, and gives him Christ's staff which he has had in his keeping. Here we have a delightful explanation for Patrick's possession of the *Baculus Jesu*, the relic, believed to have been Christ's staff, which was venerated in Ireland until its destruction at the time of the Reformation.

Patrick stays for three days on the island with that wonderful family and then proceeds to Mount Hermon, which it is stated is in the vicinity. In fact Mount Hermon, a sacred landmark which marked the north-western boundary of Israelite-conquered territory under Moses, is the highest peak on the east coast of the Mediterranean; it rises above the sources of the River Jordan west of Damascus, at the present frontiers of Jordan and Syria.

On Mount Hermon, the Lord himself appears to Patrick and tells him to go and preach to the Irish. Patrick asks three boons of the Lord: nothing less than that he shall sit at his right hand in Heaven; that he himself shall judge the Irish on doomsday; and that he shall have as much gold and silver as he and his party of nine can carry away with them, to be given to the Irish as a reward for believing.

Then Patrick goes to Rome, where he receives holy orders from Pope Celestine. Auxilius, Iserninus, and others of Patrick's party are ordained on the same day.

Finally Patrick and his companions arrive in Ireland. They reach *map, p. 69* first the harbour at the mouth of the Vartry River where, soon after landing, Patrick baptizes his first Irish convert Sinell mac Findchadha. We are told that this happened in the fifth year of the reign of King Loegaire who (as in the earlier accounts) has been warned by his soothsayers of the arrival of a new prophet who will win the hearts of the people and overthrow the ruler and his idols.

From the mouth of the Vartry Patrick sails on northwards, anchoring at the mouth of the Malahide, but not staying there as he finds no fish; he continues to Inishpatrick and the mouth of the River Nanny at Laytown near Julianstown, Co. Meath, and then to the estuary of the Boyne which he blesses because of the abundance of fish his party finds there. While they are there, a wizard mocks at Mary's virginity. Patrick makes the sign of the cross and the wizard is swallowed up by the earth.

As in Muirchú's account, Patrick finally brings his boat into *plate 2* Strangford Lough where he hides it at the mouth of the Slaney, meets, converts and baptizes Dichu and receives from him the gift of a barn.

Carrying gold with him in order to impress the man whose slave he once was, Patrick goes to the place of his former bondage to preach to Miliuc. As in Muirchú's account, the potentate commits suicide, setting fire to himself with all his treasures.

Patrick returns to Dichu's country in Ulidia where he goes about evangelizing the inhabitants. At Bright near Downpatrick, Co. Down, he meets the young swineherd Mochaoi who is converted, baptized, and tonsured. A crozier falls from Heaven and Patrick gives it to Mochaoi; the *Tripartite* thus provides a miraculous provenance for the relic subsequently venerated in the monastery founded by St Mochaoi at Nendrum, Co. Down, and known as the *Eteach* of Mochaoi.

Then, as in Muirchú's account, Patrick decides to celebrate Easter *plate 3* in the vicinity of Tara. He lights the Pascal fire on the Hill of Slane, and we are told in generally the same terms of the subsequent miraculous events at Slane and at Tara. At Slane, when the deer are seen to flee, the *Tripartite Life* puts into Patrick's mouth the words of a hymn of exultation, the *Fáed Fiada* or Deer's Cry, better known now as the *Lorica Patricii* or Patrick's Breastplate. The *Tripartite Life* also adds an exquisite miracle at Tara, in which Patrick breathes on the teardrops shed by three children at Loegaire's court and the tears are changed into gems which the children swallow. Patrick prophesies that from them will be born Columcille, Comgall and Finnian.

After the confrontation with Loegaire's wizards at Tara, Patrick orders his follower Loman, who has remained through the forty days of Lent at the mouth of the Boyne guarding their boat, to bring the vessel down river to Trim, Co. Meath, where Feidlimid, a son of Loegaire, has his stronghold. Feidlimid's son Fortchern comes upon Loman reading his Gospel. He listens, is converted and baptized. Fortchern's mother, Scoth, a British princess, comes to look for her son, finds him being instructed by Loman, and welcomes the clerics (from which we may infer that Scoth was a Christian by origin). Her husband Feidlimid comes to listen to Loman and is also converted; on land he donates Patrick founds a church, and leaves it in the care of Loman. The text states that this foundation was made at Trim twenty-five years before Patrick's foundation at Armagh. *plate 5*

From Trim Patrick goes to Teltown, Co. Meath. This was the site of Celtic assemblies and games which took place annually in August; it is also mentioned in old Irish literature as a pagan burial place named after the goddess Tailtiu. Today, as already noted, a number of earthworks can still be seen, spread over a large area of which the centre appears to have been *Rath Dubh*, the Black Fort, a circular earthwork about 150 feet in diameter and partly surrounded by a bank. Cremated bones discovered in a nearby field indicate that it, too, was a cemetery in pre-Christian times.

After Teltown, at Donaghpatrick, Patrick baptizes Conall, son of Niall, confirms him in his sovereignty and founds a church, sixty feet in length, on a plot which Conall measures out for him. Returning to Teltown, Patrick blesses the place of assembly, and then goes on his way, stopping to found churches at Ath da Laarg (*vadum duarum furcarum* – the Ford of the Two Forks) near Kells, where he leaves three of his male followers and their sister, and at a place named as 'Druim Corcotri' where he leaves a disciple, Diarmait son of Restitutus. Then Patrick returns to Tara, where Loegaire tells him of his difficulty in believing in the new faith.

Here, in the *Tripartite* account, is interpolated an event which, we are told, took place after Patrick had been in Ireland for twenty years. He goes to Rome (it is stated that, in all, he visited Rome on three occasions) and on his way meets six priests from Ireland who were on a pilgrimage. He gives them the hide satchel which he always had with him in Ireland. It was subsequently, the *Tripartite Life* relates, brought back to Ireland and embellished with gold and bronze adornment; known as the *Breifnech Pátraic,* this relic was kept, according to this account, at 'Cluain Ernáin' identified as Clonarney, in the barony of Delvin, Co. Westmeath.

We are next told the story of Patrick meeting a woman named Rigell who tells him that her husband is ill and asks him to bless her son. Patrick sains the boy and entrusts him to his disciple Cassan to be instructed. The boy, Lonan, learns to read the psalms in twelve days; he becomes the priest of a church called 'Caill Uatlech', which was later attached to the monastic *paruchia* of Clonmacnois and subsequently to that of Clonard.

Returning to Patrick's first missionary itinerary through Leinster, the account brings him next to a site named 'Tech Laisrenn' where he baptizes the men of the east of Meath and leaves two disciples, Lugaid and the nun Bice, who, when she died, we are told, was buried near Patrick's Well in front of the church which he established there. Turning southwards Patrick founds a church, 'Immliuch Sescainn', on the shore of Lough Ennell, and places in charge of it a disciple from Britain named Molué. Two other named foundations apparently in this region cannot be satisfactorily identified. On Patrick's route near Clonfad, Co. Westmeath, we are told of a miraculous hawthorn called 'Domnach'. Anyone who cut off a branch of it would be sure to fail in all his undertakings thereafter.

Patrick sets out on another expedition from Tara to Uisneach. This site in Co. Westmeath is in the fertile plain anciently called Teathba, which was the granary of Ireland. Uisneach was, traditionally, not only a royal seat but also the most important place of assembly in Ireland, where, as already mentioned, a great annual gathering took place on May Day. A number of ancient monuments can still be seen there on the hill, including burial mounds and the remains of a fort which was protected by a surrounding ditch. The stone known as 'Ail Na Meeran' (the Stone of the Divisions) on the western side of the Hill of Uisneach is believed to mark the spot where the five ancient provinces of Ireland converged. James Woods, the author of *Annals of Westmeath, Ancient and Modern* (1907), compares 'Royal Uisneach' to 'Royal Tara', explaining that what Emain Macha was to Ulster, Tara to Meath, Cruachan to Connacht, and Cashel to Munster, Uisneach was to Westmeath.

Of the two chiefs at Uisneach in Patrick's time, Enda and Fiacha, brothers of Loegaire of Tara, Enda accepts Patrick's missionary message, and the *Tripartite Life* goes on to relate his baptism by Patrick at a place in the barony of Conry, Co. Westmeath. Enda gives Patrick one ninth of his land and offers his new-born son, Cormac Snithene, to Patrick, who takes the child to be reared by four of his disciples. With other followers Patrick leaves holy relics at Leckan, Co. Westmeath.

At this juncture in the narrative we are told the story of Bishop Muinis who had accompanied Patrick on a sea-voyage from Britain to Ireland, on which occasion they had exchanged croziers. Muinis conserves the crozier which was originally Patrick's, along with other relics including a book-shrine for St John's Gospel and a bronze altar ornamented with gold, at Forgney, Co. Longford. At that place Patrick miraculously removes a lake from beside the church to a new site in Connacht because Muinis complains of the noise the warriors make when they gather there. Patrick entrusts Muinis with the responsibility of baptizing one twelfth of all the Irish, and also sends him to Rome to the Pope.

The account takes Patrick to Ardagh, Co. Longford, where he has established a church entrusted to the brothers Bishop Mel and Bishop Melchu. Patrick has received a report that Mel has had sexual intercourse with a kinswoman who shares his habitation and prays with him. Patrick discerns that there is no truth in the allegation, but advises them, so as to avoid scandal, to live apart, and she removes to another place.

Mel was traditionally a kinsman of Patrick, and died, according to the *Annals of Ulster*, in 488. Beneath the cyclopean stonework ruins of an Early Christian church dedicated to St Mel in Ardagh, excavations in 1967 revealed traces of an earlier timber building; these could be of the fifth-century church of Bishop Mel founded in Patrick's time.

In the *Tripartite Life* Patrick then proceeds to Granard. The motte of Granard, said to be the largest in Ireland, which rises above the site of the present Roman Catholic parish church at the end of the town, was not there in Patrick's time; it is an earthwork fortification made several centuries later by the Anglo-Norman invaders. An unlovely statue of the Saint, erected in 1932, now crowns it incongruously. At Granard Patrick leaves Guasacht, the son of his old pagan master Miliuc. Miliuc's daughters, the two Emers, are given the veil by Patrick and left in the nunnery founded at Clonbroney. The convent at Clonbroney is later mentioned in the Irish Annals: the *Annals of Ulster* notice the death of the Abbess St Samthann in 739; and the *Annals of the Four Masters* record the death of the Abbess Anlaith in 933.

From Clonbroney, Patrick travels across the plain called 'Mag Slecht' which stretched from Ballymagauran, Co. Cavan, to the border of Co. Leitrim. There he comes across the idol 'Cenn Cruaich' (probably *Cromm Cruaich*), the chief idol of Ireland, covered with silver and gold and surrounded by twelve other idols of brass. Patrick sends for Loegaire so that he may witness the banishment into Hell of this idol. The twelve lesser idols are caused to sink into the ground up

to their heads. Then Patrick baptizes many in a well which is named for him, and founds a church which he entrusts to a disciple, Mabran, who is his own blood-kinsman.

p. 70 Although it has no metal trappings, the stone idol at Boa Island, Co. Fermanagh, to the north of Co. Cavan where Patrick found 'Cenn Cruaich', may give us some idea of the sort of idol Patrick found. This monument, in Caldragh graveyard on the south shore of Boa Island in Lower Lough Erne, is carved with two effigies joined back to back. It has been suggested that some Early Christian stone figures found on White Island in Lower Lough Erne and now against a wall of the ruined church, are meant to represent St Patrick, King Loegaire, and Loegaire's son Enna, commemorating an incident in the *Tripartite Life* when Enna choked to death because he ate mutton at a time when Patrick was fasting to convert Loegaire. Patrick invoked the aid of St Michael to resuscitate Enna. The 'Enna' figure is depicted holding two rams wearing ritual mantles as if for sacrifice, a possible allusion to this miracle, the 'Loegaire' figure holds a small circular shield and a short sword and wears a penannular brooch. The 'St Patrick' figure is depicted with a tonsure, like that of the carving said to represent St Patrick on an Early Christian stone cross at Carndonagh, Co. Donegal; his left hand points to his mouth, his right holds a pastoral staff, and from his girdle hangs an object which appears to be a bell.

Patrick then crosses the Shannon at the ford named Swim Two Birds. At that time, long before bridges were built across the rivers of Ireland, the crossing had to be made at a ford where the waters were low. While we can no longer cross the Boyne at Trim or Slane where *plate 5* Patrick and his party forded it because the river has become too deep, we can still find the spot on the Shannon where it is most likely that Patrick crossed. North of Battle Bridge, about a mile and a half north of Drumboylan, the river runs swift but shallow, divided by a little island where it cuts through a ridge of post-glacial gravel. That there was once a ford there is attested by the presence of some much-worn stepping stones on the bank. When Oliver St John Gogarty visited the spot about fifty years ago, old people showed him the field where Patrick's charioteer died beside the ford, and, built into the floor of a house beside the ford, the flagstone on which they believed he had lain. According to local tradition too, because Patrick blessed the ford, no one was ever drowned while making the crossing despite the strong current.

Once across the Shannon, as in Tirechán's account, Patrick informs his disciples of the underground altar with glass chalices at its four angles; like Tirechán, the *Tripartite* author offers no explanation for the existence of this altar, or for Patrick's knowing of it.

At Kilmore, Co. Roscommon, in the plain of Moyglas, Patrick places Conleng and Ercleng in charge of the church he founds, and, leaving them there, goes to a spot north of Slieve Banne where he comes upon the wizards Id and Hono. Hono rejects the gift of eternal life which Patrick offers him in payment for his land, but accepts a lump of gold which Patrick finds where swine are rooting near by.

At Elphin, Co. Roscommon, where One, son of Oengus and grandson of Erc the Red, offers the Saint his dwelling, Patrick makes a well and establishes a foundation beside it. There he leaves in charge a bishop named Bite and his mother, Cipria, and his smith, Bishop Assicus, who made his altars, vessels and book-shrines. This foundation is soon followed by another at Shankhill, Co. Roscommon, where he leaves three male disciples and a nun.

After his next foundation at Tawney, Co. Sligo, Patrick arrives at the well of Cliabach (Clebach) beside Rathcroghan where the *Tripartite* account of the conversion of Loegaire's daughters, Ethne and Fedelma, agrees with Tirechán's (see pp. 55-6).

The *Tripartite* account names next a foundation at Ardleckna and others in Co. Roscommon, before bringing Patrick to Fuerty, where as in Tirechán's account his Frankish disciples leave him to continue evangelizing and to establish the church at Baslick, while Patrick founds a church at Oran.

Next we find Patrick in the vicinity of Tulsk, still in Co. Roscommon, at the Mound of the Chase, where on three stones he writes the names 'Jesus', 'Soter', 'Salvator', and in the presence of his assembled followers imparts his blessing to the Ui Briain.

On the southern shore of Lough Gara Patrick founds another church, and beside it he digs a well which will never run dry although no stream feeds it. In the same neighbourhood about four miles south-west of Boyle, Patrick makes a foundation for the nun Athracta who has been professed and clothed by him. Before leaving Athracta at Killaraght Patrick blesses her veil and gives to her a chasuble which falls miraculously from Heaven. This nunnery and its first abbess gave the parish there its name, Killaraght. The nunnery was to flourish for centuries; a hospital, traditionally established by St Athracta, beside it, existed until the Reformation, and an abbess is mentioned at Killaraght as late as 1591.

After pursuing the sons of Ercc who steal his horses, Patrick reaches the barony of Costello in Co. Mayo. As in Tirechán's account, we read of the foundation at Mucno's Well, of the cross standing where Secundinus (Sechnall) had stood, and of Patrick's next foundations in the baronies of Kilmaine and Carra. Patrick foils an attempt on his life by a slave sent to assassinate him and retires into the wilderness for two Sundays.

At Aghagower, Co. Mayo, where he leaves a bishop named Senach to care for the foundation, Patrick puts two salmon into the well beside the church to live there for ever.

On the Saturday of Shrovetide Patrick reaches the great cone-like
plate 6 mountain known familiarly to the Irish as 'the Reek'. This is Croaghpatrick, whose summit commands a view to the Twelve Pins of Connemara, across the more-than-three-hundred islets of Clew Bay to Achill and to Cahir Island, Inish Turk and Clare Island in the Atlantic, to Nephin, and, beyond Slieve League, as far as Donegal. Fields of heather clothe the lower slopes of the reek, but beyond the heather-bells and the saxifrage loom gaunt grey-green, stony heights which are not, as they appear to be, the apex of the cone, but a high plateau, now crowned by a chapel.

On that summit, the *Tripartite* tells us, Patrick wrestles with an Angel who appears to him there to tell him that God will not grant him all that he asks for because his demands are both excessive and obstinate.

'Is that God's pleasure?' asks Patrick. The Angel confirms that it is. To this comes Patrick's surprising reply: 'Then my pleasure is that I shall not leave this reek until I am dead or until all my requests are granted.'

Disheartened, Patrick remains on Croaghpatrick from Shrove Saturday to Easter Saturday, abstaining from both food and drink. As to Moses, God speaks to Patrick out of a fire.

At the end of forty days and nights a vast swarm of blackbirds covers the place where Patrick is, so that he cannot see. The birds do not leave even when Patrick sings maledictive psalms at them; growing angrier, he strikes his bell loudly, flings it at the birds and so breaks it. Patrick weeps copiously, his tears soak the front of his chasuble; an Angel who comes to console him dries his chasuble. White birds come to fly around them singing sweetly, and the Angel promises Patrick the sea and land as far as his eye can see. Patrick asks, 'Is there nothing else that He grants me besides that?' The Angel tells him that he may have seven souls saved from Hell on every Saturday until Doomsday. Patrick replies that if God is going to give him anything, let Him give twelve souls. 'Thou shalt have them but get thee gone from the reek,' says the Angel. Patrick refuses to go, saying that as he has been tormented he will not go until he is satisfied, and asks what else God will give him. The Angel promises the rescue from Hell of seven souls every Thursday in addition to the twelve already promised every Saturday, if Patrick will leave the reek. Patrick again refuses in the same terms; he asks what else he can have. The Angel reveals that a great sea is to flood over Ireland seven years before the Judgment, and again asks Patrick to be gone from the reek. Again Patrick refuses. 'Is there aught else thou wouldst demand?' the Angel asks him. 'There is,' says Patrick, 'that the Saxons should not dwell in Ireland by consent or by force as long as I abide in Heaven.' The Angel promises exemption from pain and torture to all who sing Patrick's hymn from one watch to another. When Patrick complains that the hymn is long and difficult, the Angel emends the requirement to singing the hymn from '*Christus illum*' to the end only, and adds that anyone who gives anything in Patrick's name, and all who make penitence in Ireland, shall escape Hell. Yet again, the Angel tells Patrick to leave the reek, and yet again Patrick refuses. The Angel promises Patrick the rescue, on Doomsday, of one soul for every hair on his chasuble. Still Patrick refuses to obey the Angel's injunction to leave the reek, remarking that he will not accept this blessing, as any one of the saints who labour for God could expect to bring so many souls into Heaven.

The Angel asks Patrick what he will accept. 'That is not hard to say,' Patrick replies, 'seven persons out of Hell on Doomsday for every hair on my chasuble.' The Angel, not yet fully exasperated, grants this, and for the sixth time tells Patrick to leave the reek. When Patrick refuses this time the Angel threatens him with force, but Patrick boldly answers that even though the High King of Seven Heavens should come, he will not leave until he is fully satisfied, so the Angel asks him what else he wants. Patrick asks that on the Day of Judgment he, himself, should judge the people of Ireland. The Angel tells him that assuredly that blessing cannot be obtained from the Lord. 'Unless it is got from Him,' Patrick says to the Angel, 'there is no way that I shall leave the reek before Doomsday.'

The Angel goes back to Heaven. Patrick celebrates Mass. The Angel returns at the ninth hour to relay to Patrick God's message. It is that after the twelve Apostles, there would be no man more admirable than he, were it not for his hardness, but that nevertheless he may have what he asked for. Patrick is to strike his bell, and when a heavenly shower falls on him, go down on his knees; the people of Ireland living and dead will be consecrated to him, at which Patrick exclaims, 'Blessed be the bountiful King who has bestowed; now shall be the departure from the reek.'

Patrick celebrates Easter at Aghagower. His charioteer is buried in the neighbourhood, between the Reek and the sea. Patrick founds three churches in Partry, Co. Mayo, and baptizes many thousands there. He is told that a certain well is honoured by the pagans as if it were a god, the King of Waters, so he and his neophyte Cainnech, the founding bishop of Carra, Co. Mayo, remove the stone which covers the well.

Following the story of Patrick resurrecting the swineherd who had been dead for one hundred years, we are told of Patrick's custom of going up to every cross on his travels, even if this necessitated leaving his immediate road. On one occasion he omits to visit a cross on his route, only because he does not know that it is there. At eventide, when his charioteer informs him of his omission, Patrick leaves his meal and his resting-place and goes back to the cross. While praying at the cross he discerns that it is the site of a grave, and asks who is buried there. The corpse's voice answers him from the tomb: 'A wretched heathen am I. I was buried here. While I was alive I fell while injuring my soul and I was buried here.' Patrick then asks why the Christian symbol of the cross marks the grave. The corpse tells him that it was erected there in error by a woman who mistook the place for her son's grave. Patrick then realizes why he had unwittingly passed this cross. He removes it and sets it up in its rightful place over the grave of the Christian woman's son.

When Patrick's charioteer cannot find their horses in the dark, the Saint raises his hand and, as if they were so many lamps, his five fingers light up the whole plain so the horses are found.

Patrick crosses the River Moy to Tirawley, Co. Mayo, where the twelve sons of Amalgaid were contending for the kingship. The twelve set out in chariots for Tara so that Loegaire can adjudicate the issue. The haughtiest of the brothers excludes his eldest brother's son, Conall, from the arbitrage because he is too astute. Outside the stronghold Conall encounters Patrick, who tells him how he heard the voices of the Irish children calling him to come back to Ireland. When Patrick learns that Conall has been shut out, he tells him to enter, that the doors shall open for him. He is to go to Eogan who is a faithful friend and, secretly, take his fourth finger, that being a token between them.

Conall pleads his father's case successfully with Loegaire. Oengus is enraged and incites two others of the brothers to murder Patrick and Conall as they pass through the barony of Corran, Co. Sligo. On the spot, these brothers refuse to kill the two innocent men. Oengus comes to a place which came to be known as the Wizard's Hill, near Killala, Co. Mayo, with bands of men and two wizards, one of whom promises that as soon as he looks at Patrick, the Christian will be swallowed up into the earth. The reverse happens. As he is being submerged, the wizard gasps that he will believe if he is saved; he is flung up into the air and lands on the ground half-alive. He believes, and is baptized. The other wizard, less fortunate, is flung into the air and falls down to smash his head on a stone and be consumed by heavenly fire. The *Tripartite Life* tells us that the spot is marked by the wizard's stone and by a church named Cross Pátraic.

Ruan, the blind son of Amalgaid's charioteer, comes to Patrick desiring to be healed. When one of Patrick's followers laughs at the blind man, Patrick tells him that for this, it were meet that he, instead, should be blind. Ruan is healed, and Patrick's disciple who laughed loses his sight.

Two lame men who appeal to Patrick are healed. Still in the neighbourhood of Killala, at a well to the west of Cross Pátraic, Aed the Tall, a grandson of Oengus, is healed of lameness by Patrick. Nine wizards who seek to kill Patrick are consumed by heavenly fire.

The well-preserved Round Tower at Killala may mark the exact site of the earlier monastic foundation established there by Patrick, and entrusted by him to its first bishop, Muiredach. There Patrick meets, according to the *Tripartite Life*, two sisters Crebriu and Lesru, whom he had once seen in a vision calling him from their mother's womb to come and evangelize the people of Ireland.

At Farragh near Killala, Patrick baptizes the monarch Amalgaid and several of his sons. However one of Amalgaid's sons, Oengus, vows that he will not become a believer until he sees his long-dead sister Fedelma brought back to life. Patrick resurrects Fedelma from her grave, along with the male child which was in her womb when she died; he baptizes Fedelma and the infant. Fedelma expounds to the people on the pains of Hell and the reward of Heaven, and beseeches her brother Oengus to believe in God through Patrick. Oengus is baptized in the same well as his sister. Twelve thousand others of the people of Amalgaid from the forest of Foclut hear and believe.

As Oengus owns land in the neighbourhood of the necropolis of Loughdall, Patrick goes there hoping that he may be given it for a foundation. However, Oengus' conversion has only been superficial, and when he comes to meet Patrick he is drunk. Patrick prophesies that all Oengus' descendants will be drunkards and parricides.

At Kilmoremoy near the present border of the counties of Mayo and Sligo, Patrick erects a stone cross; and there, at a ford over the stream near the church, he baptizes a man and resurrects the man's dead wife.

The Moy must rank among the most attractive of Ireland's many beautiful rivers. Near its banks now stand the lovely ruins of two *plate 9* fifteenth-century Franciscan friaries, Moyne and Rosserk. After seeing a girl drown in the estuary of the Moy Patrick prophesies that no one shall ever drown there again. Looking across the river and the sandhills to Bertragh, he prophesies that that region shall be his. He curses people who stone him and his followers, and prophesies that they shall never win in any contest and shall, forever, be mocked in any assembly which they attend.

On his way eastwards into the tribal territory of the Ui Fiachrach, Patrick curses a flood which hinders his progress. In the stronghold called 'Caisel Irre', a fort at Killaspugbrone near Sligo town, Patrick gives to the bishop, Bron, one of his teeth. The *Tripartite* author assures us that in his day a flagstone in the hall of the fort marked the spot where the Saint's tooth fell. The tooth was long preserved there, so that Killaspugbrone became a centre of pilgrimage. The Shrine of St Patrick's Tooth, the *Fiacal Phádraig*, made in the fourteenth century to hold the relic, is now in the National Museum, Dublin.

At Carrowmably, near Easky, Co. Sligo, three poison-giving wizards overtake Patrick, but are unable to harm him. Patrick tells fishermen to cast their nets into the river that runs through Sligo town. They tell him they will do so, because it is he who bids them, but that no salmon have ever been caught there in winter. They catch great salmon in their nets and present them to Patrick, who blesses the river with abundance.

Warriors on Patrick's route try to terrify him and his followers by making a din with their spears and shields. Patrick curses them that they and their children shall always be defeated in battle. But when five of the men kneel before him, he modifies the curse and tells them that whenever they shall be routed, notwithstanding how many of the enemy might pursue them, no more than five of them shall fall.

The next incident has Patrick on his way to Moylurg, Co. Roscommon. He falls into the River Boyle and curses the river to the east of the ford, which thereafter yields very little fish, while the waters to the west remain fruitful. In Moylurg he curses the people because his horses are stolen by the sons of Ercc, but attenuates the curse at the request of the bishop, Maine, who bathes Patrick's feet with his tears and dries them with his own hair.

Patrick goes from Drumlease, Co. Leitrim, eastwards into the glens where, in his time, the *Tripartite* author tells us, a flag-stone still marked the spot where blood fell from the Saint's nose. In Rossinver parish, at Sraud, Patrick founds a church, and then continues on his route past Drumcliff, Co. Sligo, a place now more renowned for its elaborately sculpted but weathered High Cross erected about the year 1000, and also as the burial-place of the poet W.B. Yeats.

Crossing the plain between the Erne and the Drowes, Patrick blesses the River Drowes because of the kindness shown to him by boys who are fishing in the river. The lovely little Drowes was famed thereafter for its salmon, among the finest in Ireland. *plate 8*

At Assaroe in Co. Donegal the local magnate sends men to expel Patrick, but their attempt to do so is not successful; the man who sets his dog on the Saint is cursed along with his heirs, and Patrick prophesies ill-luck for the magnate. Continuing on his way between Assaroe and the sea Patrick marks out a site for a church at Racoo near Ballyshannon, and another which he prophesies will be a princely seat. At Mullaghshee, Conall, son of Niall, receives a prophetic blessing from the Saint, who blesses all of his lands and strongholds and announces that a wonderful youth will be born of his sept. The *Tripartite Life* explains that this was, in fact, St Columcille.

Patrick passes through the narrow Barnesmore Gap between high mountains into the barony of Raphoe, where he establishes a church at Donaghmore. There he warns his disciples to beware of the ruler Eogan, son of Niall. One of Eogan's sons, Muiredach, is promised the reward of kingship if he can prevail on his father to believe. Eogan comes to Patrick, and believes. He complains to the Saint of his ungainly appearance, and when Patrick asks him how he would like to look, replies that he would like to look like a youth named Rióc from Inishboffin who carries Patrick's box. Patrick covers Eogan and Rióc with one mantle and they fall asleep clasped in one another's arms. When they awake they have exactly the same form, except for Rióc's tonsure. Then Eogan tells Patrick that he is dissatisfied with his height, too, and would like to be taller. Immediately he grows to the height he has indicated with his upraised weapon. Patrick blesses Eogan and his three sons. Muiredach and his heirs are rewarded with kingship, the heirs of Fergus are to be priests, the heirs of Eochu are to be warriors.

Patrick's next stopping-place was the great royal stronghold, the Grianán of Aileach, which commands a magnificent view over Lough Foyle and Lough Swilly. It was the seat of the chief of the powerful Ui Néill from the fifth century. Three concentric stone ramparts, a part of the original fortification, remain, surrounding the fine stone fort which dates from Patrick's century but suffered in the internecine wars of later centuries, and was restored just over a century ago. The enclosed area of the fort is seventy-seven feet in diameter; the walls which are no less than thirteen feet thick contain chambers in their thickness.

The *Tripartite Life* recounts that Patrick gives his blessing to the fortress. He leaves a flagstone there and prophesies that both secular and ecclesiastical rulers over Ireland would come out of the place.

After blessing all the peninsula of Inishowen as far as Malin Head (the most northerly point of Ireland where there is now a meteorological station), Patrick founds seven churches along the River Faughan. Of these, three are identifiable as Clooney in Co. Derry and Bodoney and Donaghedy in Co. Tyrone.

Patrick returns to Inishowen. Just west of Moville, now a small resort town on the Inishowen peninsula, a lane climbs to Cooley where there is a slender, ancient stone cross, ten feet in height. Local tradition has it that an impression on the rectangular stone base of this cross is St Patrick's footprint. The *Tripartite Life*, however, does not specifically mention this place. It has Patrick at Magheradrumman where he establishes a hermitage.

Returning from Inishowen to Co. Tyrone, Patrick ordains three bishops there, one of whom is placed at Tullyleek in the parish of Donaghmore. Seven churches are established in the barony of Keenaght, Co. Derry; three of these are named, of which one is identifiable as Duncrun in the parish of Magilligan.

Heading eastwards, Patrick crosses the River Bann into a region where it was the custom of the inhabitants to fish by night. Patrick orders the men to fish by day. His route takes him into the northern part of Antrim through the ancient kingdoms of Dalaradia and Dalriada.

A local monarch in those parts tells Patrick he hears the cry of an infant from under the ground. A cairn at the place is demolished, and when the grave is opened an odour of wine issues from it. In the grave is the corpse of a woman who died of ague, and beside her an infant born after her death and still living, having survived beside his dead mother in her tomb for seven days. Patrick baptizes this child, the future Bishop Olcán of Armoy in Co. Antrim.

Patrick establishes churches and cloisters in Dalriada, at Ramoan, at Culeightrin, at Grange of Drumtullagh, at Drumeeny. At Dunseverick on the northern coast of Co. Antrim, the northern end of a route from Tara in Celtic times and a point of embarkation for Scotland, Patrick blesses a site and makes a well.

Patrick acquires further sites in Dalaradia; one at Glenavy, Co. Antrim, is mentioned particularly because of its curative well, and because there Patrick curses Sarán who tries to drive him away, and deprives him of both Heaven and Earth. This wretched man's brother, however, offers land to Patrick at Comber in Co. Down, and in return he is blessed to be the progenitor of kings and princes for ever.

Other identifiable Co. Antrim Patrician foundations named in the text are on the Islandmagee peninsular between Larne Lough and the sea; at Rashee in the barony of Antrim Upper; at Glore in Glenarm, the oldest of the Antrim glens villages on the east coast at the foot of the glen of that name; and at Glynn in the barony of Lower Belfast. The ancient church near the footbridge across the Glynn river in that picturesque village is believed to be on the site of Patrick's foundation.

Next the *Tripartite Life* tells how Olcán, the child rescued from his mother's tomb but now already a bishop, pleads for the liberation of slaves held captive by Patrick's adversary Sarán at Glenavy. In return for their freedom, Sarán wishes to have restored to him Heaven of which Patrick deprived him. Olcán explains that it is beyond his power to grant what Patrick has taken away, but when Sarán threatens to slay all the captives, Olcán, hoping to save their lives, promises Heaven to the tyrant. Patrick learns of this and is enraged. Olcán and Patrick meet at Clonfeacle, a few miles north of the city of Armagh, where Patrick orders his charioteer to drive right over Olcán. When the charioteer demurs on the grounds that he dare not mow down a bishop, Patrick lays a curse on the man's earthly goods, but tells him that his merit will be exalted in Heaven. Sarán's guilt is imputed to the unfortunate Olcán.

A brother of Sarán donates a site at Coleraine to Patrick. Patrick's prophecy that this foundation will belong to both his own heir and the donor's is eventually fulfilled in the person of Coirbre, the donor's grandson, consecrated by a bishop who had been consecrated by Patrick.

Patrick brings with him, out of Dalaradia, Guasacht and the two Emers, the son and daughters of Miliuc (Milchu) his master when he was a slave. He leaves the kingdom via Toomebridge where the Lower Bann flows out of Lough Neagh. The fame of this village now is the largest eel-fishery in the British Isles, managed by a co-operative of about four hundred local fishermen and farmers.

Patrick comes into the territory of the Ui Tuirtri where he remains for forty days, at a spot near the southern shore of Lough Neagh, somewhere between the Lough and Slieve Gullion which has been called 'Ireland's most mysterious mountain'.

Patrick wishes to found a cloister there, but he is opposed by the local ruler who orders him to leave. Patrick curses his adversary and deprives him and his heirs of the territory in favour of the ruler's brother who, with his pregnant wife, is blessed and baptized. She gives birth to a daughter, Trea. When this Trea becomes a nun, Angels bring the veil for her from Heaven, and clothe her with it when she is professed by Patrick. Patrick blesses the veil, after which Trea never raises it for the rest of her life.

Seven churches founded by Patrick in the territory of the Ui Tuirtri are named in the *Tripartite Life,* and two can be identified; one is at Donaghrisk, a townland in Dungannon Upper barony, Co. Tyrone, and the other at Donaghenry in the same county. The men of one tribe living to the west of Dungannon refuse Patrick's message, but he blesses and baptizes the men of another tribe in the same region, and leaves with them a priest, Columb, and also his own book of ritual and bell.

After visiting Tullamain in Co. Derry, Patrick turns southwards to found churches and cloisters in the barony of Slane in Co. Meath.

From there it appears that Patrick returned to what is now the province of Ulster, for we hear of him next on the road to Clogher in Co. Tyrone with his disciple, the son of Cairthenn who becomes Bishop there. Clogher is still the seat of a bishop, and although now little more than a village, it is proud of its ancient history and its tradition that the diocese was founded by Patrick; the Protestant Cathedral is dedicated to Patrick's disciple, St MacCartan, the first Bishop of Clogher. We know that in Patrick's day Clogher was a place of some importance. Excavations on the hill-fort of Rathmore behind the cathedral have revealed traces of its Iron Age inhabitants, including decorative metalwork from Roman Britain, Patrick leaves at Clogher a relic called the *Domnach Airgit* which he had received from Heaven when he was on his way to Ireland.

On a hill at Findermore, a townland in the barony of Clogher, Patrick preaches for three days and three nights. By a miracle his listeners feel that he has only preached for one hour; however, Brigit, who is present, falls asleep during this marathon homily. Patrick does not disturb her, but afterwards asks her what she has seen. Brigit tells him that she has seen assemblies of people all robed in white, light-coloured oxen, and white cornfields with, behind them, speckled oxen and black oxen; that after this she has seen sheep, swine, wolves and dogs, all quarrelling, then a small stone and a large stone, the smaller of which grew in size and emitted silvery sparks when a shower fell on them, while the larger one wasted away. Patrick explains this vision to Brigit. The two stones represent the two sons of Echaid, one of whom accepts Christianity and is blessed while the other does not and is cursed.

The next event concerns Cinnu, the daughter of the ruler named Echu whom Patrick raises from death. Echu wants his daughter to marry Cormac, a man of suitable family-background. Cinnu, however, is a baptized believer, and she has heard from Patrick of the joy of a spiritual union with the Heavenly Bridegroom. Patrick asks Echu to permit Cinnu to become a nun. Echu agrees to give his consent if he is allowed, in return, to attain Heaven himself without having to be baptized. Patrick promises this, although, we are told, it is difficult for him to do so. Cinnu takes the veil, joins Patrick's retinue, and is sent to a cloister to be instructed by the nun Cechtumbar. When Echu reaches the end of his life he tells those who are with him not to bury him until Patrick shall come; as soon as he has uttered these words he dies. Patrick is at Saul in Co. Down where Echu's death is revealed to him. He sets out for Clogher, arriving only twenty-four hours later. In a scene very reminiscent of the New Testament,

Patrick enters the house where the corpse lies and tells the mourners to leave. Falling to his knees, he weeps and prays, and then commands Echu, in the name of Almightly God, to arise. Echu rises; he sits down and speaks. The mourners rejoice. Patrick instructs Echu in the faith and baptizes him. At Patrick's bidding Echu then expounds to the people on the pains of Hell and the joys which the obedient enjoy in Heaven. Patrick then allows Echu to choose between living another fifteen years on earth peacefully in full enjoyment of his royal position, or going at once to Heaven. Echu replies that even if the kingship of the whole world were granted him, he would count it as nothing in comparison with the blessedness that had been shown to him, and that he chooses absolutely to leave the sorrows of the world and return to the everlasting joys of Heaven which he has seen. Patrick commends Echu's soul to God, and he dies.

At Tehallan in the barony of Monaghan, Patrick leaves a bishop and some aged disciples, and entrusts to their care relics that he brought from abroad. Three men steal one of the two goats that carry water for Patrick, kill it and eat it. When questioned by Patrick they deny what they have done, but the goat bleats in their bellies and exposes their perjury. Patrick curses the thieves that goats will thenceforth cleave to their descendants.

The King of Omeath where Patrick has blessed and baptized the inhabitants, beseeches Patrick to resurrect his dead grandfather, Muiredach. Patrick complies. Muiredach is resurrected, baptized, and then re-buried.

In the barony of Cremorne, Co. Monaghan, when a man named Victor, on hearing of Patrick's arrival, hides himself in a thorn thicket, the thicket is miraculously illuminated at night; Victor emerges and submits himself to Patrick. Rather astonishingly the Saint immediately bestows a church on Victor: Donaghmoyne, a parish in the barony of Farney between Carrickmacross and Castleblayney.

Still in the barony of Farney, Patrick rests on Sunday at Killaney about two miles from Carrickmacross on the road to Dundalk. The inhabitants of the place give Patrick poisoned cheese to eat, but as soon as the Saint blesses the offered food the cheeses are turned into stones. The author of the *Tripartite Life* asserts that these stones could still be seen at the place.

The people who tried to poison Patrick at Killaney pursue him with a band of horsemen as he journeys southwards, hoping to trap him at a ford and slay him. From a hillock to the south of the ford Patrick turns towards his pursuers and, with his left hand raised, prophesies that they will drown in the fort and remain beneath its waters until Doomsday. In fact, when they try to cross, the waters do sweep over them and they are all drowned.

At Coole in Lower Kells barony, Co. Meath, Patrick blesses the inhabitants; he establishes a foundation which is subsequently attached to the community of Ardbraccan. Continuing southwards Patrick sleeps at Dunmurraghill, Co. Kildare, and reaches Naas, where he pitches his tent in the green of the ruler's fort and baptizes his neophytes in a well to the north of it. Patrick summons the reeve of the fort but the man feigns sleep. When Patrick is told, he exclaims that it will not surprise him if this is the man's last sleep. Indeed, when the reeve's men return to the fort to awaken him they find him dead.

After Naas, Patrick is in eastern Wicklow, where it seems that he has gone because Dricriu (the monarch of a region in Newcastle barony, married to a daughter of Loegaire) is holding a feast at a fort, which evidently stood at a harbour named 'Rath Inbir'. Dricriu refuses to invite Patrick to the feast; however the Saint is welcomed by another of the Ui Garrchon, who kills his only cow and gives him his share. The man's pregnant wife cooks for Patrick, who blesses the couple and their unborn child.

Patrick founds churches and cloisters in the plain of the River Liffey, at Killashee in the barony of Naas, where he appoints Auxilius, and at Kilcullen, Co. Kildare, where he leaves Iserninus and another disciple.

On Patrick's route westwards, young boys from Leix lay a trap for him over concealed pits filled with water at Moone in Co. Kildare. When he reaches the place, the boys urge him to drive on, crying 'For God's sake, drive on your horses.' Patrick orders his charioteer, 'Drive on your horses for God's sake.' Miraculously, no harm befalls the Saint, but he lays a curse of unceasing persecution, complaint, and foreign domination on the people of Leix. Because a woman of the Ui Ercain named Brig had informed Patrick of the snare which was prepared, her people are blessed and promised dignity, riches and independence.

At a church not far from Sletty in Slievemargy barony, Co. Leix, Patrick asks Dubthach maccu-Lugair for a comely well-born young man with only one wife who has not yet had a child. Dubthach replies that unfortunately the bard Fiacc, who answers this description, is away in Connacht. However, Fiacc arrives at that moment. Dubthach schemes to be tonsured himself, but Fiacc offers to take his place and Patrick chooses Fiacc, who is at once baptized, tonsured and made Bishop of Leinster. Patrick presents Fiacc with a bell, a crozier, and other sacred objects, and leaves seven of his disciples with him to settle on a foundation two miles north of the town of Carlow on a site which, with the sites of thirty or forty other churches in Leinster, had been donated by Patrick's convert, the magnate Cremthann.

Fiacc's original foundation was on the east side of the River Barrow, but after an angelic warning he moved to Sletty on the west bank of the river, where the community flourished. It was there, under Bishop Aedh who died in 699, that Muirchú pursued his Patrician studies and wrote his *Life of St Patrick*. The monastery at Sletty was plundered in the ninth century but survived the attacks, the last mention of an abbot there being the obituary of the Abbot Maelbrighde in 1055. Little is left now on the site of this once-flourishing monastery. There are two primitive, tall, undecorated granite crosses which appear to date from the Early Christian period, and some remains of a medieval church.

On a Sunday, when he is at a church established in the plain near Morett, Co. Leix, Patrick forbids some workmen to dig the earthworks for a royal fort on the sabbath. As the men do not heed him, the Saint prophesies that unless the sacrifice of the Mass is offered there every day the stronghold will be unstable.

Patrick's route takes him through the Gowran Pass into Ossory, where he founds churches and cloisters. At Kells in Co. Kilkenny, where there are now the extensive remains of a once-magnificent Augustinian Priory, Patrick leaves sacred relics in the care of some of his disciples who remain there.

On the way into Munster, the axel of Patrick's chariot breaks. Two others made on the spot from local timber break also. Patrick declares that no building shall ever be made from the wood of that grove; the *Tripartite Life* tells us that this prophecy was fulfilled, and not even a skewer was made from timber from that place.

When Patrick arrives at the imposing royal seat on the Rock of Cashel, the monarch Oengus son of Natfraich awakes in the morning to find that all the idols have fallen on their faces. Oengus welcomes Patrick and his retinue, and invites them to come into the fort. The sons of Natfraich are baptized by Patrick, and he blesses the men of Munster. While Patrick is baptizing Oengus the spike of his crozier impales the monarch's foot. When Patrick perceives what he has done, he asks Oengus why he made no murmur of complaint. Oengus replies that he took the piercing of his foot to be some rite of the new faith. To recompense Oengus, Patrick promises him that none of his descendants will ever die from a wound. Patrick promises that future monarchs at Cashel shall be consecrated as bishops also; the author of the *Tripartite Life* adds that, thereafter, twenty-seven king-bishops of the family of Oengus ruled at Cashel until Cenngecán. This is the name of a king-bishop of Cashel who was slain in 897.

The Rock of Cashel which rises dramatically above the surrounding plain was an important royal site before Patrick's time, having been a fortification of the kings of Munster by the fourth century, but with the conversion of the monarch it became a seat of both secular and ecclesiastical power, and the scene of many historic happenings. The famous Irish monarch Brian Boru was crowned on the Rock in 977; his descendant King Muirchertach O'Brien gave the Rock to the Church in 1101. The King-Bishop Cormac MacCarthy built the exquisite Romanesque church which still stands *plate 10* on the Rock; it was consecrated in 1134. The Round Tower is of about the same date, but the ruined cathedral dedicated to St Patrick was built mostly in the thirteenth century.

The conversion of the King of Munster was, of course, an outstanding success for Patrick, a high moment in his missionary career. According to the *Tripartite Life* the Saint remained in Munster evangelizing for seven years. From his triumph at Cashel he goes on to found churches and cloisters in the barony of Clanwilliam, Co. Tipperary. One day as he washes his hands at a ford, one of his teeth drops out and falls into the water. Patrick climbs a hill to the north of the ford and dispatches some of his followers to look for the tooth; they find it without difficulty because, miraculously, it shines in the water like the sun. The place is named, thereafter, *Ath Fiacla* (the Ford of the Tooth) and the church which Patrick founds, and in which he leaves the tooth with four of his disciples to care for the foundation, is called *Cell Fiacla* (the Church of the Tooth). The modern name of this place is Kilfeakle, Co. Tipperary, a modest village on the main road from Cashel to Tipperary town, where the river and hillock of the *Tripartite* narrative may be seen.

Patrick's route continues westwards, to the barony of Coonagh in eastern Co. Limerick and the neighbourhood of Cullen in the adjacent barony of Clanwilliam, Co. Limerick. He reaches a hill-top encampment where he meets the local magnate, Ailill.

Near Cullen is a hill where an impressive standing stone still rises *plate 11* above the remains of an ancient rath, and it appears that this must be the place where Ailill's wife comes to tell her husband that their son has been devoured by swine. Ailill tells Patrick that he will become a believer if Patrick can bring the boy back to life. Patrick tells them to gather the boy's bones together, and then he directs one of his disciples, Malach, who is from Britain, to bring the boy to life.

Malach's faith fails him; he excuses himself by saying that he will not tempt the Lord. Patrick prophesies that Malach's cloister and community will never flourish. (In an aside, the author confirms that this prediction came true – Malach obtained a foundation at Kilmaloo in the barony of Decies-within-Drum, Co. Waterford, where the pasture would hardly feed five cows.)

Patrick then calls upon his disciple Ailbe, and a bishop named Ibair to bring the boy's bones back to life, and he joins them in prayer. The boy is resurrected, and preaches to the crowds. Ailill, his wife, and their people, the Ui Cuannach, all believe and are baptized. Patrick forgives and even blesses four men who steal his horses.

Ailill's pregnant wife is stricken with a deathly disease. She tells Patrick that she has seen in a vision a herb which is the only thing that will cure her. Patrick asks her to describe the appearance of the herb, and she tells him that it was like rushes. Patrick blesses some rushes which turn into a leek. Ailill's wife eats it, is healed, and gives birth to a son. Patrick is said to have declared: 'Omnes femine quaeque de illo holere manducaverint sanae erunt.' (All women who shall chew this vegetable will be healthy.)

There are a number of hills around Galbally, Co. Limerick, at the head of the lovely Glen of Aherlow, so it is not possible to identify the rath near Galbally where two magnates Corbre and Broccán try to prevent Patrick from sojourning, but the top of Duntryleague hill, where there are remains of primitive earthworks and a fine megalithic tomb, seems likely to have been the place in question. Patrick eventually acquires the place he wants for a foundation despite the opposition of Corbre and Broccán.

Another magnate, Dola, also opposes Patrick in his desire to sojourn at his stronghold near Grean (Pallasgrean). Patrick prophesies that Dola's stronghold will be diminished to a miserable place, abandoned by all but two or three people living in slavery or wretchedness, and that all the others will emigrate. However, as the women of Grean had accepted Patrick's message and lament his departure, the Saint gives them his blessing and extends it to any children they shall bear to men of a tribe other than Dola's.

Patrick establishes a church on a hill in the barony of Coonagh, at Kilteely, where the inhabitants slay two of his disciples while they are asleep. The two are buried there. The site of this event may have been a hill now known as 'Cromwell's Hill', which rises to 580 feet and commands an extensive view across the county as far as the estuary of the Shannon. On its summit is a prehistoric burial cairn known as 'Diarmid and Grainne's Bed'.

Patrick goes into the territory of the Ui Fidgente, where a banquet is prepared for him. When a troupe of jugglers ask Patrick for food, he refers them to those responsible for the feast, but they are refused food by the local magnate and by Patrick's deacon who is helping to prepare it. However, a youth named Nessán arrives with a cooked ram on his back and gives it gladly to the jugglers, who are immediately swallowed up into the earth. Patrick predicts that neither secular rulers nor bishops will come of the ungenerous magnate's progeny, while the deacon's cloister will be modest and frequented by the rabble. The generous Nessán is baptized, ordained a deacon, and a church is founded for him at Mungret, Co. Limerick. Nessán's mother who, for fear of the magnate, expressed her disapproval of Nessán giving the meat to the jugglers, is fated to be buried apart from her son.

The Annals record a death-date for St Nessán of Mungret in 551. If we may assume that he lived to be eighty, he would have been born about 471, and could have been 'a youth' in the 480s, towards the end of Patrick's life and mission. The monastery at Mungret flourished and is said to have had a community of 1,600; it survived Viking raids in the ninth century but was subsequently plundered by Irish chieftains. The ruins of two early churches may be seen on the site of the ancient foundation.

The men of North Munster who come by ship to meet Patrick are baptized. He blesses them for their generosity to him from a hilltop which (we are told) commands a view of the country to the north of Limerick. This was probably the peak of the volcanic rock called Knockpatrick, which does command a superb view over the Shannon estuary and its environs.

At Singland, now a built-up suburb of Limerick city, Patrick baptizes people, and the miracle of the birth of a son to the wife of Cairthenn is celebrated; hitherto she had given birth only to stillborn children. The infant is named Echu Redspot because of a red spot on his body, a reminder that he was miraculously fashioned by Patrick from a drop of blood.

Patrick blesses the land around Limerick and the islands in the Shannon estuary. He does not, the text tells us, then go westwards over the mountains into Co. Kerry, but southwards into the barony of Coshlea to found a church and cloister at the place now called Ardpatrick, Co. Limerick. There the local magnate, Derball, challenges Patrick to move the Ballyhowra mountains so that he would be able to see as far as the barony of Fermoy, saying that then he would believe. Patrick melts a pass through the mountains, which are

plate 12

clearly visible from the windswept hill above Ardpatrick, but he warns Derball that he will have no profit from his demand, nor any monarch or bishop of his progeny, but every seventh year the Munstermen will peel him like an onion.

A monarch who delays in coming to greet Patrick offers the excuse that he has been held up by the rain. Patrick prophesies that when this man's people gather in assembly it will shower. The Saint curses a stream in which he loses some of his books, and he curses the fishermen who fish the stream because they reject him.

On reaching the River Suir, Patrick blesses it and the surrounding land to be fruitful. He evangelizes in the baronies of Lower and Upper Ormond where he promotes to the rank of kingship one of twelve brothers who comes to meet him, while the other eleven all arrive late. One of these late-comers offers the excuse that he was delayed because he was erecting a fence. Patrick prophesies that the descendants of this man will never manage to fence in and enclose their dwellings entirely because their earthworks will crumble, their fences will fall and their crannógs (small artificial islands in the lakes or at the marshy edges of lakes) will disintegrate. Others who come late with excuses receive appropriate punitive prophecies.

When Patrick finally leaves the province of Munster, after founding churches and cloisters, performing ordinations, healing the sick, and raising the dead, he is followed as far as Brosna in Co. Offaly by a devoted crowd of men, women and children. At Brosna he resurrects a Munster man who has been dead for twenty-seven years. Patrick's followers from Munster attend a feast which he blesses, at Creevagh, Co. Offaly, and there, with renewed benedictions, he bids them farewell.

From Creevagh, Patrick's route turns eastwards to the territory of the Ui Falgi, a region on the eastern border of Co. Offaly which extends into the barony of Offaly in Co. Kildare. There, a devotee of the idol Cenn Cruaich (which Patrick had destroyed earlier on his mission in Co. Cavan) boasts that he will kill Patrick in vengeance. However, Patrick's charioteer changes places with the Saint in the chariot, and it is he who is the victim of the murderer. The villain is cursed, dies, and goes immediately to Hell.

9 Patrick's traditional route along the shores of Killala Bay in northern Mayo was hallowed by later ecclesiastical foundations, such as the now-ruined Franciscan friary at Rosserk, which flourished in the 15th century but fell into disrepair after the Reformation

12 A church is said to have been founded by St Patrick himself on the windswept hill at Ardpatrick in Co. Limerick. The ruins seen here are of an Early Christian church. The magnificent site at the northern edge of the Ballyhowra mountains commands an extensive view

Previous pages: 10 On the Rock of Cashel, where tradition has it Patrick preached and baptized the ruler of Munster, the ruins of the medieval cathedral and earlier Round Tower rise to form a dramatic skyline

11 The earthworks of a prehistoric dwelling-site and the standing stone near Cullen are visible reminders of the pagan population who lived there before the dawn of Christianity. This site is one of the magnate's strongholds visited by Patrick, according to the *Tripartite Life*

Returning into Ulster, Patrick encounters on his way some slaves who have been left to fell trees. In order to make them suffer the more, their master does not allow them even to sharpen their tools, so that their hands bleed from their exertions. Patrick goes to the tyrant and pleads for the slaves, but to no avail. Patrick curses the cruel slave-owner and, when he goes to beat his slaves to punish them for having voiced a complaint against him, his horses drag him and his chariot into a lake. The tyrant's widow comes to Patrick to repent, and kneels before him; he blesses her womb and her two sons are baptized. Patrick predicts that her son Iarlaith will be one of his successors.

For the remainder of the narrative, which tells of events occurring at unspecified times during Patrick's mission, he is in the south-east of the present province of Ulster, or just across its border in what is now Co. Louth.

One Sunday, Patrick is sleeping near the sea at a place called Drumbo where he is disturbed by a noise of pagan workmen digging a rath. He asks them to cease their noise, but they ignore his request and mock him. Patrick prophesies that their work will come to naught. This prophecy proves very soon to be true. The next night there is a tempest; the sea comes up and demolishes the earthwork.

The monarch Echaid binds two maidens and leaves them on the strand to be washed over by the sea because they have vowed to be nuns and have refused to marry or worship idols. Echaid refuses to heed Patrick's entreaties in behalf of the girls, so Patrick curses his inheritance, and the kingship passes to the descendants of Echaid's brother. However, Echaid's pregnant wife, who kneels at the Saint's feet, receives his blessing, and he blesses her unborn child.

At Drumcar in Ardee barony, Co. Louth, an Angel tells Patrick not to continue with the cloister which he has begun to build there, for it is not the place where he must abide. Patrick asks where he is to settle. The Angel tells him that Armagh is the appointed place. Patrick looks wistfully at the meadow below him and remarks how fair it is. The Angel tells him that it shall be called '*Clúain cáin*' (Fair meadow), and that a British pilgrim will come and establish himself there, and it shall be a part of Patrick's *paruchia*. The place is the parish of Clonkeen in Ardee barony, Co. Louth, where there was a monastery until at least the latter years of the ninth century.

At Ardpatrick, Co. Louth, where he wishes to establish a cloister, Patrick blesses the people who have followed him. Each day he goes to meet his disciple Mochtae at a place between Ardpatrick and Mochtae's own foundation at Louth, where an Early Christian stone church stands on the site of Mochtae's first church. One day an Angel places a letter between them, telling Mochtae to remain at his own foundation, and Patrick to be obedient and to proceed to Armagh. Patrick leaves in Mochtae's care the twelve lepers who are housed at Ardpatrick, and Mochtae goes there every night to give them their food.

In obedience to the Angel, Patrick goes to Armagh. He arrives at the rath of a rich magnate and asks him for a site for a church, but he is not given the great hill he aks for (the present site of the Protestant Cathedral), but another site (where, in the time of the author of the *Tripartite Life*, there was a cemetery). Patrick establishes a church there, and remains at the place for a long time. One day the magnate sends two of his horses to graze on the church lands. Patrick is enraged and the horses die immediately. The magnate's ghillie reports to his master that the Christian has killed his horses because they were grazing close to the church, so he orders his ghillie to drive Patrick out. However, the magnate falls deathly ill; his wife forbids the explusion of Patrick and tells her husband that his illness is due to his treatment of Patrick, to whom she sends to ask for holy water for her husband. Because of the wife's belief, Patrick sends the holy water; it is sprinkled on the magnate and his horses and restores them all to life and health.

The grateful magnate sends Patrick the gift of a copper cauldron. The story of how the Saint accepted it and how the magnate was offended is as told by Tirechán, culminating in Patrick's acceptance of the cauldron and of the site he had always wanted at Armagh.

Ercnat, a daughter of the magnate, falls in love with Patrick's disciple Benen (Benignus). She falls ill and dies. Benen takes her remains to Patrick. The Saint resurrects Ercnat, who thereafter loves Benen spiritually and without physical desire.

Ten virgin princesses, nine of them daughters of a king of the Lombards, and one of a king of Britain, come on a pilgrimage to Patrick. They stop near Armagh and send messengers to ask Patrick whether they may meet him. He replies that three of them shall go to Heaven and be buried on the spot where they are staying, while others are to go to a place named as 'Druim Fendeda', One of them, Cruimtheris, is to establish herself on a certain hillock called 'Cengoba', east of Armagh. Every night Benen takes her food there, on Patrick's instruction. The nun Cruimtheris has a lapdog which drinks doe's milk. Patrick has an apple tree transplanted from the fort to the field where this doe grazes; thereafter the field is known as 'Aball Pátraic' (Patrick's Orchard).

Patrick rests one night by a well. The Angel awakens him. Patrick asks the Angel if he has done anything to anger or offend God. The Angel assures him that he has not, and that he alone is to have spiritual dominion in Ireland. Patrick replies that he would like those who succeed him to be honoured by God also. The Angel tells him that God has given him all Ireland and every free man that lives there. Patrick gives thanks to God.

Patrick is angry with his own sister Lupait because she has committed the sin of lust and become pregnant.

The author of the *Tripartite Life* seems here to have been quite unconcerned with the chronology of Patrick's life, and whether the sister, who is said to have been abducted with him when he was a youth, would have been of a likely age to become pregnant at a time when Patrick had been a missionary in Ireland for many years. Albeit, we are told that as Patrick approaches the church, Lupait falls to her knees beside his chariot, and Patrick commands his charioteer to drive over her. The charioteer drives over Lupait three times. Her remains are interred by Patrick with a sung requiem.

Lupait has pleaded with Patrick in favour of the man who has had intercourse with her and is the father of her child, Aedan. He is Colmán, son of Ailill of the Clanbrassil, a tribe in the barony of East Oneilland, Co. Armagh. Patrick grants Lupait's request not to deprive Colmán and his progeny of Heaven, but he prophesies that they will always be sickly.

At a place where Angels remove a stone from the road on the route of Patrick's chariot, he raises his hands and blesses Armagh. Holding the *Baculus Jesu* in his hand, preceeded by an Angel, and followed by his companions, Patrick surveys his enclosure, presumably the stronghold at Armagh. He lays a curse on anyone who shall sin therein, and a blessing on those who will do God's will there. He then measures out the lengths of the burial ground – one hundred and forty feet, the great house – twenty-seven feet, the kitchen – seventeen feet, and the oratory – seven feet. We are told that these became the standard measurements of Patrick's cloister everywhere.

The remains of the ancient stronghold of Eamhain Mhacha or Emania, now more usually known as Navan Fort, two miles west of Armagh, consist of earthworks on a low drumlin hill. The large, roughly circular enclosure of about eighteen acres is surrounded by a broad bank and a ditch. Excavations at the fort, which occupies a key position in the Heroic legends, have revealed evidence of Early Iron Age occupation. According to the *Tripartite Life* it was at Eamhain Mhacha that God appeared to Patrick in the form he will have on the

Day of Judgment. The effect of this apparition on Patrick is so awful that he flees to the south, reaching in only one day the confluence of three rivers, the Barrow, the Nore and the Suir, in the south-east of Ireland, a journey which is the best part of a day's drive at reasonable speed in a motor car today.

The relics kept at Armagh are explained by a journey to Rome that Patrick made when he travelled from Ireland in a boat which came from Bordeaux to fetch him. All the inhabitants of Rome fell asleep while Patrick was there, so he was able to carry away as many relics as he wanted. With God's blessing he brought three hundred and sixty-five relics to Armagh, including relics of Peter, Paul, Laurence and Stephen, a sheet stained with Christ's blood, and a hair of the Virgin Mary.

A load of wheat which falls from Heaven, like manna, on a hermitage, is loaded and brought to Patrick. On the way, when a grain of wheat falls from the load, Patrick's horse, who is pulling it, at once lies down and will not move until Patrick arrives.

Patrick sends horses yoked to a chariot but without a charioteer from Armagh to Fiacc at Sletty. Miraculously the horses reach Mochtae's foundation in Co. Louth, where they make their first stop; from there they continue the next day to Sechnall's foundation at Dunshaughlin, Co. Meath; on the next day they find their way to Auxilius' foundation at Killashee in Co. Kildare, and finally reach Sletty, where Fiacc who is incapacitated by an insect bite on his leg is badly in need of the chariot to accomplish his Lenten penitential journey to a hilltop where he fasts.

Sechnall asks Patrick when he should compose a hymn in his honour, and the Saint tells him that it would be inappropriate. Sechnall replies that he is not asking whether it should be done, but when it should be done. Patrick, knowing that Sechnall will be the first bishop to be buried in Ireland, and will soon leave this world, tells him that the hymn should be composed without delay. After the hymn is composed, when Sechnall encounters Patrick he tells him that he wants him to hear a hymn of praise composed for a man of God. Patrick's name is not mentioned in the early part of the hymn, but it lauds a human who is 'greatest in the Kingdom of Heaven'. Patrick asks Sechnall how that is possible, but Sechnall answers evasively. The two repair to a place apart near the River Lagan to hear the rest of the hymn, and in due course Patrick hears his own name. Sechnall asks what shall be his reward for the hymn. Patrick grants blessings to all who recite, before death, the last three chapters, lines, or even words of the hymn with a pure intention (see pp. 39-40).

Patrick learns that Sechnall has said that he, Patrick, is an excellent man save for one thing. The Saint asks Sechnall what this is, and Sechnall points out to him respectfully that he rarely preaches charity. Patrick replies: 'It is for charity that I do not preach charity, for if I preached it I should not leave a yoke of a pair of chariot horses for any one of the saints in this island, present or future, but unto me would be given all that is mine and theirs.'

A religious couple bring butter and cheeses made of curds to Patrick for the young boys of his community. A wizard tells Patrick that he will become a believer if Patrick can change the cheeses into stones. Patrick does this. The wizard then asks Patrick to change the stones back into cheeses. Patrick complies. The wizard asks Patrick to change the cheeses once again into stones and once again Patrick complies. The wizard yet again asks for the stones to be changed into cheeses; this time Patrick refuses, saying that the stones will remain so, as a commemoration of the miracle. The wizard becomes a believer. Patrick flings his little iron hand-bell into a dense thicket. Patrick has prophesied that a servant of God will come to the place. Dicuill arrives. He finds the bell and the stones which were cheeses. The author of the *Tripartite Life* confirms that in his time the bell and two of the stones were at the oratory founded by Dicuill in Faughart parish, Co. Louth, while the third stone was in the church of a monastery in Co. Monaghan.

When the time of his death is approaching, Patrick prepares to go to Armagh to die and be buried there. The Angel Victor appears to him and tells him that Armagh is not the place appointed for him to lie until his resurrection, but that he must return to the Barn (Saul, Co. Down), for that is where he should die, adding that Patrick's pre-eminence, his piety, and his teaching will live on at Armagh as if he were alive. Patrick laments that he loves the Hill of Armagh, and that it is there that he had chosen to await the resurrection; but he acknowledges that he is powerless, without a choice, that he remains a slave to the end of his life.

The Angel gives Patrick instructions for his burial. His body is to be drawn in a little cart by two young oxen. The oxen are to be left to take their burden where they will, and wherever they choose to stop, that shall be his burial place. Before dying, Patrick receives the Eucharist for the last time from a bishop named Tassach. When he dies, according to the *Tripartite Life*, his body is duly put in a cart which the oxen bring to Downpatrick and he is buried there without *p. 106*
pomp. For twelve nights of vigil after Patrick's death, while hymns and canticles are sung for him throughout Ireland, there is no night

in Lecale but only an angelic radiance. The narrative adds that according to some accounts this radiance lasted in Lecale for a year after Patrick's death.

The Ulidians, the Ui Néill, and the men of Oriel contend for Patrick's body. The Ulidians wish it to remain in their territory. By a miracle the Ui Néill are prevented from disturbing the Saint's remains and removing them to Armagh.

The canon of Patrician legend does not, of course, close with the *Tripartite Life,* which, like the earlier *Lives,* makes no mention of the now most famous miracle attributed to the Saint – the apocryphal story of Patrick banishing the snakes from Ireland, a miracle which so captured the popular imagination that it is one which has been frequently depicted in stained-glass windows, and on banners and other memorials in honour of St Patrick. In fact, there never were any snakes in Ireland; their absence is due to the fact that they and other slow-moving creatures did not reach Ireland before it became an island, when the morainic land-bridges which linked it to Britain were submerged, several thousand years before St Patrick's time.

Between sixty and seventy books about St Patrick are known to have been in existence in pre-Viking Ireland, and are said to have perished in the Viking raids. By the twelfth century, when Jocelin of Furness wrote his *Life of Patrick*, the Patrician legend was reaching its fullness of growth; further miracles were attributed to the Saint, holy wells attributed to him proliferated, even in parts of the country not mentioned in any of the earliest itineraries, and forged Patrician documents were already in circulation. It was in the late twelfth century that a legend of a cave in Ireland offering the experience of Purgatory spread abroad, capturing the imagination of contemporary writers and drawing intrepid pilgims to visit the supposed site of the entrance to the underworld. The enduring attraction of Purgatory, and the wonderful and terrifying experiences reported by the visitors there, are the subject of the following chapter.

The first 'modern' biography of St Patrick, written by Richard Stanihurst, was published at Antwerp in 1587, but Stanihurst, like other sixteenth-century antiquaries, was uncritical of his sources. Philip O'Sullivan Beare's *Patriciana Decas,* published in Madrid in 1629, is a more erudite work but still uncritical in its use of source material.

The first truly critical account of Patrick's life was the work of the scholarly Protestant Primate of Ireland, James Ussher (who included it as Chapter XVII in his *Antiquities of British Churches* in 1639).

Ussher corresponded with an expatriate Irish Jesuit on the Continent, Father Stephen White, who like Father Henry FitzSimon, hunted for and found early texts of Irish interest in libraries and repositories in Germany and Belgium. Ussher also had access to a manuscript of Jocelin's work (now in Trinity College, Dublin), to a collection of fourteenth-century hagiographies in the *Codex Kilkenniensis* which he himself owned and annotated, and, what was more important, he consulted the *Book of Armagh* itself and perused the Patrician documents it contained.

For about two hundred years Primate Ussher's work remained the only critical study of Patrick's life and the source of all quotations from Tirechán. Other seventeenth-century historians like Father John Colgan in Louvain relied on Ussher's work, as did the Bollandists, who also included a text from the St Vaast Codex of the *Confessio* and the *Letter to Coroticus* in their notice of St Patrick in the *Acta Sanctorum*.

It is in the nineteenth century that we find a renewal of historical interest in Patrick's life and the legends. Dr John Lanigan treated the subject in the first volume of his *Ecclesiastical History of Ireland* in 1822. Muirchú's text had not then been published, and Lanigan pleaded for Boulogne-sur-Mer in France as Patrick's birthplace, and while he dismissed Jocelin's work (which had been published in an English translation by Edmund Swift in 1809), he was not successful in dating the earlier sources. Professor Ludwig Bieler has aptly described Lanigan's approach as being 'on the borderline of old and new scholarship'.

More influential was *St Patrick, Apostle of Ireland*, by the Rev. James Henthorn Todd, published in 1864, but the author was biased in his efforts to establish that Patrick was the true precursor of the Established (Protestant) Church of Ireland, leading Roman Catholics to view his work with suspicion and to reject zealously any criticism of even the more fanciful miracles. Indeed the corpus of popular tradition was strengthened and enriched by uncritical works issuing from Roman Catholic authors like Father Morris, who even reinstated Jocelin and Probus as valid sources in his *Life of St Patrick*, and the Nun of Kenmare (M.F. Cusack) whose *The Life of Saint Patrick, Apostle of Ireland,* published both in Ireland and by the Catholic Publication Society in New York in 1869, was an immensely popular book with evocative illustrations and Celtic Revival ornamentation. In those days of heady, intransigent nationalist sentiment, the image of St Patrick as the 'National Apostle' and as a symbol of Irish nationalist aspirations was furthered by two other

Roman Catholic authors, Canon O'Hanlon in his *Lives of the Irish Saints* and Archbishop Healy in his *Life and Writings of St Patrick*, published in 1905, and these works provided the basis for most sermons on the Saint on his feast day.

Nevertheless, serious scholars were laying the ground for a critical appreciation of the sources. Father Sylvester Malone, a lone champion of historicity in the Roman Catholic camp, published a collection of critical essays in 1892, while the Jesuit Father Edmund Hogan had edited the complete texts of Muirchú and Tirechán in 1882. Other documents in the *Book of Armagh* and an original Irish text of the *Tripartite Life* were published by Whitley Stokes in 1887.

Father Gaffney's *The Story of St Patrick for Boys and Girls* was immensely popular and helped to preserve the image which had been moulded of Patrick as a national and Catholic hero.

The Protestant public, however, read Todd, which had the merit of an attempt to depict the background of pagan Ireland and the Early Christian Church there, while Roman Catholics remained happy with the works of their own writers, and the works of the critical scholars were confined to an academic readership.

The period which followed in the twentieth century saw academics pitted one against the other in the proposition and demolition of theories which ranged from doubt of the very existence of Patrick, to the suggestion that there were two Patricks whose lives and deeds had been confused — or mounting a defence of the traditional Patrick in the light of critical research. The general public, puzzled by the hypercriticism of the scholars and unable to follow many of their arguments, preferred as reading-matter Father Francis Shaw's *The Real St Patrick*, published by The Catholic Truth Society, or Mrs Thomas Concannon's pious and popular *Saint Patrick, His Life and Mission*, published in 1931.

It is, however, thanks to the questions raised by von Pflugk-Harttung and Heinrich Zimmer, and to the Patrician scholarship of J. B. Bury, Newport White, Dr John Gwynn, Father Paul Grosjean, Professor Thomas O'Rahilly, Professor Eoin MacNeill, James Carney and Dr Kathleen Mulchrone (whose works on the subject are listed in the Bibliography), and above all to Professor Ludwig Bieler whose *The Life and Legend of St Patrick, Problems of Modern Scholarship* was published in 1949, that we can appreciate the figure and personality of St Patrick as he emerges from a critical reading of the earliest sources, and in the light of historical evidence and archaeological discoveries.

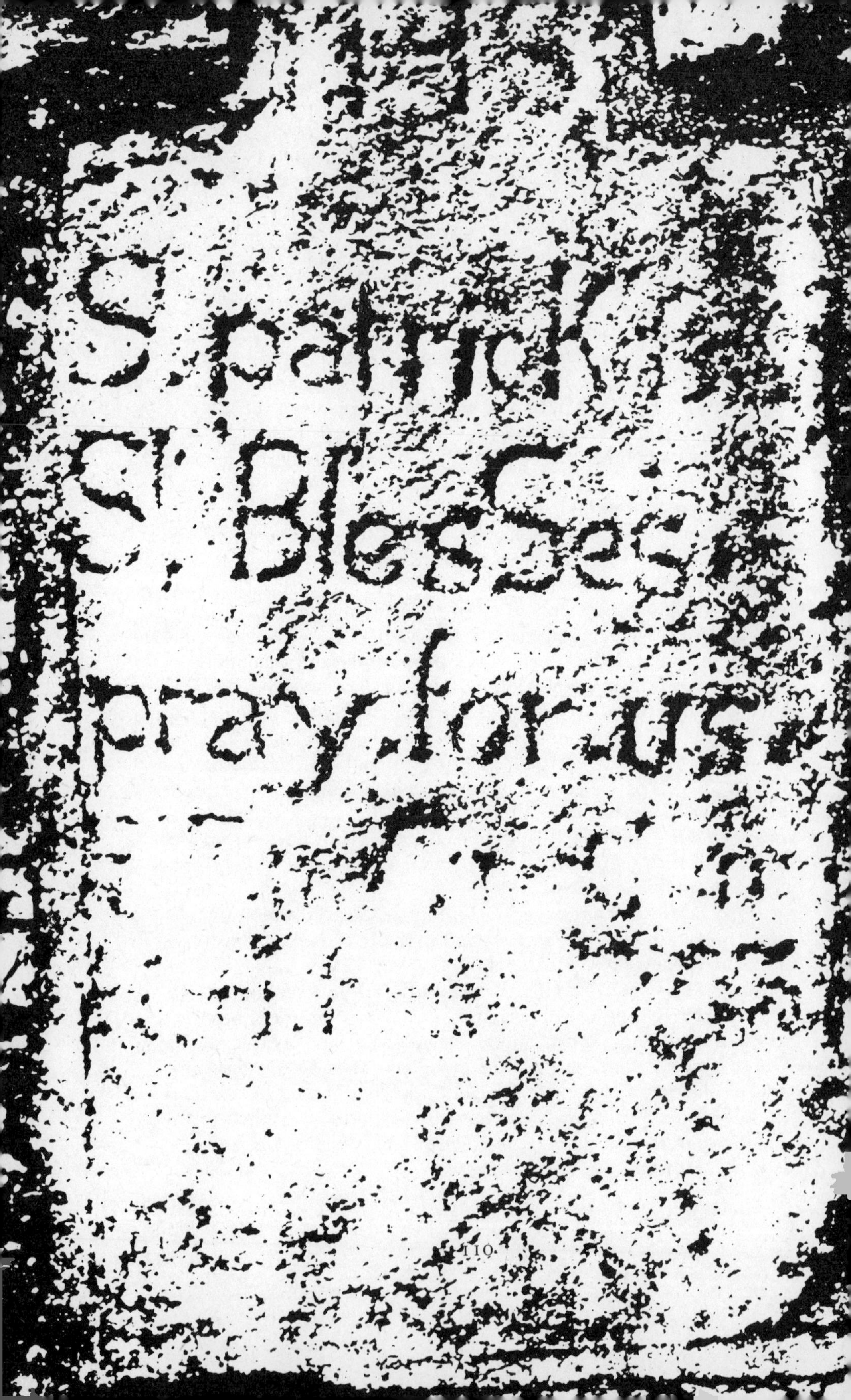
S. patrick
pray for us

VII
Saint Patrick's Purgatory

Not one of the early *Lives* of St Patrick mentions Lough Derg, or the Saints' Island cave there, famed throughout medieval Europe as an entrance to the underworld and the place where Patrick was vouchsafed a vision of Purgatory. The earliest tradition of such a cave can be traced to the latter half of the twelfth century, when an Anglo-Norman Cistercian monk, Henry of Saltrey, wrote a tale that he claimed he had heard from a monk named Gilbert. This Gilbert had been to Ireland and recounted the existence of the entrance to Purgatory upon his return to England. Henry of Saltrey tells us that he sought confirmation of Gilbert's extraordinary account, consulting among others an Irish bishop whom he called 'Florentianus'. Lough Derg lay at the meeting point of three dioceses, one of which was Derry. It would appear that the bishop in question was either Florence – Flaithbhertach – O' Broclan, Abbot and Bishop of Derry, who died in 1175, or Florence – Flaithbhertach – O'Carolan who became Bishop of Derry in 1185. According to Henry of Saltrey, the Bishop confirmed that the cave was in his diocese and that the stories told about it were true.

Belief in the cave as an entrance to Purgatory was thus established in Ireland before it became famous abroad at the end of the twelfth century. A hagiographer of St Coemgen described the 'Cave of St Patrick in Ulster' as one of the chief pilgrimages in Ireland. Jocelin of Furness, however, who wrote a *Life of St Patrick* in Latin in 1185, believed that the Purgatory was on top of Croaghpatrick, and reported that pilgrims who spent the night there suffered the most grievous tortures which, they believed, cleansed them of their sins. That Giraldus Cambrensis included an account of the Purgatory on Lough Derg in his *Topographia Hibernia*, written in 1200, implies that by this date the place already had an established reputation:

> There is a lake on the bounds of Ulster containing a double island. The one part has a Church of approved religion. It is very lovely and beautiful. It has been made incomparably glorious by the visitation of Angels and the visible

throng of the local Saints. The other part has nine Pits, in any of which, should someone dare to spend the night (which has been proved and recorded of daring men at times), he is immediately seized by evil spirits and is tortured all night with such heavy pains, and tormented so incessantly with so many grievous and unspeakable torments of fire and water, that with morning there is scarcely any or only the dregs of life surviving in his wretched body. They say that if anyone endures these torments under an injunction of penance, he will not undergo any further pains in the world below unless he has committed fresh sins. The place is called St Patrick's Purgatory by the natives.

Henry of Saltrey embellished the story he had heard and published it as his *Tractatus de Purgatorio S. Patricii*, a work which was immensely popular at the end of the twelfth century. Roger of Wendover in his *Flores Historiarum* of 1188 included a modified version of Henry of Saltrey's narrative on the Purgatory. A fellow monk, Mathew Paris, included Roger of Wendover's version in his *Chronica Majora*, compiled at St Albans. By about 1190, Henry of Saltrey's tale had been translated into a rhyming lay of over two thousand verses by Marie de France as *L'Espurgatoire de Seint Patriz*.

Henceforth the fame of the dreadful Cave on an island in Lough Derg was assured. Its appeal and fascination endured throughout the Middle Ages, nourished periodically by the reports of their fantastic experiences there by pilgrims who had entered it. Frequently these reports were circulated accompanied by certificates of authenticity from the ecclesiastical authorities. Later, the popularity of the place even survived the Age of Reason and the dismissal of the superstitious beliefs attached to the Cave. Even after the original cave was demolished and the site of the 'Purgatory' and the pilgrimage transferred to the smaller Station Island, pilgrims continued to flock to Lough Derg. Today, pilgrims still go to Lough Derg, seeking, not the horrors of approaching Purgatory but the profound consolation which they find in the rigorous spiritual exercise of penitential fasting, abstinence and prayer.

plate 13

The legend's widespread popularity is not hard to understand. Henry of Saltrey's narrative had all the ingredients to appeal to the medieval mind, attracted by the notion of intercourse with the world beyond the tomb, and fascinated by the heroic, the fantastic, the macabre, by death and corruption, and especially by the gruesome details of the horrors of damnation. This reached its strangest manifestation in the late thirteenth century with the poem '*Le Dit des Trois Morts et des Trois Vifs*', whose theme recurs in one of the illustrations of the *Très Riches Heures* of the Duke of Berry, and which gave rise to the 'Dance of Death' in which men dressed as skeletons and performed a masque.

Purgatory was defined in the twelfth century by St Bernard, who explained that after this life there were three regions: Hell from which there was no escape or redemption, Purgatory where there was hope, and Paradise. It was not clear whether all the dead who had not been thoroughly wicked would have to pass through Purgatory, or only those between the elect and the damned who had not adequately atoned on earth for their misdeeds. It was generally accepted that the purgation would be either by the heat of fire or by extreme cold, worse than anything imaginable on earth, and that the souls undergoing this painful purification would be able to glimpse visiting angels and saints, giving them assurance of salvation when their process of purging was done.

The Last Judgment was the subject of some of the most splendid, and at the same time the most gruesomely horrifying works of art in the Middle Ages. Condemned souls were shown in dreadful torment among serpents and toads, writhing between the horns of beasts and demons, burning in fire, trembling, groaning in their agony. Yet apart from the imagery inspired by Dante's *Divina Commedia*, in which Purgatory has a profound spiritual significance, there are few depictions of the state between Paradise and Hell. This did not denote a lack of interest, but rather, that to the medieval mind the conditions prevailing in Purgatory were little different from those of Hell, save for the consolatory sighting of angels and saints. A fourteenth-century English mystic, Mother Juliana of Norwich, wrote of her ardent desire for a full vision of both Hell and Purgatory, and popular English legend told of a chaplain who had been vouchsafed a vision of Purgatory. He saw flames and sulphurous fumes on one side, the frost and ice of cruel cold on the other. The inhabitants of this Purgatory were in varying degrees of nakedness or clothing, according to the degree of their sins and repentance before death.

It was generally believed that acts of penance on earth could obviate or reduce the period of purgatorial suffering. Prayers and pious endowments were considered useful, but pilgrimage was one of the temporal penitential acts believed to be most efficacious in the remission of time in Purgatory. Little wonder, then, that the cave on the island in Lough Derg attracted so much interest, combining as it did the benefits accruing from a pilgrimage and the grisly attractions of a sight of the purgatorial horrors.

Henry of Saltrey's readers were simple believers. They were not concerned that the hero of his *Tractatus*, Knight Owen, originated in the person of Ywain, one of the Arthurian Knights of the Round Table, who had appeared in the story of Ywain and Gawain in Chrétien de Troyes' *Chevalier au Lion.* Few who read of Knight Owen's experiences in the *Tractatus*, or in Marie de France's lay, or in later retellings, doubted that Knight Owen was an historical personage, or questioned the literal truth of his account of his penitential pilgrimage to Saints' Island, his descent into Purgatory through the door of the Cave and his struggle with demons in a wilderness where neither sun nor moon ever shone. Suffering the alternating agonies of searing heat and biting cold, Owen had witnessed the most awful punishment of souls – some gnawed by serpents, some hung in red-hot chains, some suspended from hooks by the sinful members of their body, some roasting on spits, or boiling; others impaled on a wheel, plunged into molten metal, or driven naked into an icy lake. Knight Owen returned from his horrifying experience, unlike other penitents, many of whom, it was related, entered the Cave and never came back.

And why should the readers have doubted the least part of the story, when the very Cave of the story of Knight Owen (below) was there to be visited? The situation of the Cave, on an island in a remote lake, in Ireland which was then the western extremity of the known world, only rendered the story of its being the entrance to Purgatory more likely, more feasible.

Attracted by the account of Knight Owen's penitential experience, a steady stream of real penitents went to Lough Derg. There, after a period of fasting and prayer, and due warning and dissuasion by the Prior, if the penitent pilgrim still insisted, he was locked in the Cave overnight.

Accounts of the Purgatory proliferated. By 1245 its fame was sufficient for Maître Gossouin to include a report of the place in his *L'Image du Monde*. If the Augustinian canons who guarded the cave had commissioned publicity to attract penitents and the intrepid curious, they could not have hoped for better than this:

There is another place in Ireland which is called the Purgatory of St Patrick, which burns like fire day and night. It is so perilous that none go there who are not well confessed and repentant. Sometimes they are ravished and lost and it is not known what becomes of them. If he is confessed and repentant he passes through many torments and purges himself of his sins. The more sins he has committed the more griefs and torments he has to undergo. When he returns from this Purgatory he will never again take pleasure in the sights of the world and he will never laugh again but he remains weeping and groaning for the sins people commit and for the evil he sees them do. In this Island there is a great mountain of sulphur which burns day and night.

By the latter half of the thirteenth century St Patrick's association with the Purgatory had been firmly established, as is shown by the account of Jacobus de Voragine (given here in Caxton's translation):

On a time as St Patrick preached in Ireland the faith of Jesus Christ and did but little profit by his predication for he could not convert the evil, rude and wild people: and he prayed to our Lord Jesus Christ that he would show them some sign openly ferdeful and gastful, by which they might be converted and be repentant of their sins. Then by the commandment of God St Patrick made in the earth a great circle with his staff and anon the earth after the quantity of the circle opened and there appeared a great pit and a deep, and St Patrick by the revelation of God understood that there was a place of Purgatory, into which whosoever entered therein he should never have other penance nor feel other pain and there was showed to him that many should enter which should never return nor come again. And they that should return should abide but from one more to another and no more and many entered that came not again. As touching this pit or hole which is named St Patrick's Purgatory some hold opinion that the second Patrick, which was an Abbot and no Bishop, that God showed to him this place of Purgatory, but certainly there is such a place in Ireland wherein many men have been and yet daily go in and come again and some have had there marvellous visions and seen grisly and horrible pains, of whom there have been books made …

For a first-hand account of experience in the Purgatory of St Patrick we must wait until the fourteenth century and the *Visiones Georgii, Visiones quas in Purgatorio Sancti Patricii vidit Georgius Miles de Ungaria.* The pilgrimage of the Hungarian Knight, George, was attested by the Primate, Richard FitzRalph, Archbishop of Armagh from 1347 to 1360, and by Nicholas MacCathusaigh, Bishop of Clogher from 1320 to 1356, who granted George the necessary licences to enter the Cave.

George had crossed France and England on foot to reach Lough Derg in 1353. Upon his insistence he obtained the necessary ecclesiastical permissions. He then made his confession and fasted on coarse bread and water for fifteen days. For five days he lay like a corpse in a black-draped bier in the church, while the Office for the Dead was recited for him morning and evening by the canons wearing funerary vestments. After this, accompanied by the Prior and canons and by the local chieftain and nobles, George was led into a small chapel where he saw a door which he described as like one used for a cellar; it would seem that he meant a trap-door. Miraculously, George was able, without help, to move three massive stones which had been placed in front of this door and which, the Prior attested, had blocked it for thirty years. The Prior opened the door with the key and blessed George, who was barefoot and bareheaded, robed in three loose white tunics. As George began the descent of a twisting stair, a splendid and priceless Cross of St Patrick which was attached by a strong cord was placed in his hand, and he continued downwards into a deep pit. George returned safely from his descent, in the course of which he went not only into Purgatory, but to Heaven and Hell also. He brought back secret messages which he had received from the Archangel Michael (whom he had seen face to face) to be delivered to the Primate of Ireland, to Edward, King of England, to the Queen Mother of England, to King John of France, to Pope Innocent VI and to the ruling Sultan of Babylon and Egypt.

Five years after George, Louis, a French knight from Auxerre, left a record of his adventure in the Purgatory of St Patrick, where, among other experiences, he was tempted by beautiful women who sang and danced to enchant him, wearing gorgeous apparel and jewelled crowns.

Gruesome accounts of these and similar experiences continued to be related periodically by traveller-pilgrims from England and continental Europe. It was usual for those who experienced the horrors of Purgatory to lead a life of extreme penance and abstinence on their return from Lough Derg. A returning pilgrim from Brederode in the

Netherlands, for instance, is reported to have entered a Benedictine monastery, which he helped to endow, as well as building a chapel dedicated to St Patrick. Undoubtedly, the devotion to St Patrick at diverse places in Europe was frequently due to a pilgrimage to the Purgatory.

Viscount Ramon de Perelhos, a Spanish nobleman in the service of the Pope at Avignon, set out for Lough Derg in September of 1397, ostensibly to ascertain the state of the soul of his late monarch, King Juan I of Aragon, who had died in the preceding year. Armed with a letter of safe conduct from King Richard II of England, the Count was received in Dublin by Roger Mortimer, Earl of March and Ulster, the Lord Lieutenant, and at Drogheda by the Primate, John Colton, Archbishop of Armagh. Both tried to dissuade him from continuing his journey, but he remained determined and reached Lough Derg. There, with the help of the local chieftain, he went out to the island. He entered the Cave and passed fearfully through its depths, devoid of light, until he came to the place where sinful souls were being punished by fire, by cold water, by being impaled on the spokes of a wheel, or suspended, and by other tortures. He found there, not only the late King of Aragon whom he sought, but deceased friends and connections of his own, including a kinswoman who had been alive when he left for Lough Derg, and of whose death he was unaware. This unfortunate lady was lingering in Purgatory to be punished chiefly for having spent so much time painting her face.

William Staunton, a pilgrim from the diocese of Durham in the north of England, came to Lough Derg in 1409. He was the first to relate that he was assisted in Purgatory by celestial guides. According

to Staunton's account, he fell asleep after entering the Cave, and on awaking found before him a man in the white habit of a canon and a woman in white wearing a nun's veil. Introducing himself, the white-clad monk said, 'I am clept in North country John of Bridlington and so I am, and this woman is Saint Ives my sister that lived in Quittock.'

The Augustinian John of Bridlington, who died in 1379, had been canonized by Pope Boniface IX in 1401, only eight years before William Staunton's pilgrimage to Lough Derg. John's own shrine at Bridlington was then a popular centre of pilgrimage, and it is likely that Staunton, whose home was not many miles away, had been there. Already in his childhood John of Bridlington had made himself remarkable by his extreme piety and precocious prudence. Miracles were attributed to him – that, by prayer, he had caused empty granaries to be replenished, that he walked on water, that he raised the dead. Within a few years of his death John was popularly honoured and worshipped in England as a saint, and his official canonization increased his fame.

Accompanied by St John of Bridlington and St Ives who were ministering to the souls in Purgatory, William Staunton encountered his own deceased sister. Later he was conducted to a strongly walled house reserved for the imprisonment and punishment of sinful clergy, who were fed on worms pushed into their mouths by fiends, or pelted with great hailstones, or forced to wear doublets which mysteriously pained them. Before returning to the world, Staunton was allowed to ascend a ladder to the top of a tower whence he had access to a portion of Paradise. There the earth was as clear as crystal, the trees

were the fairest he had ever seen, and the scent which came from them was so exquisite that he could only say that it was sweeter of savour than all the spicers' shops in the world. In the trees, wonderful birds sang delectable songs. The souls William encountered in Paradise congratulated him on his good deeds performed on earth, and on his lucky escape from the perils and grisly sights of Purgatory.

Two years after William Staunton, a Hungarian nobleman went into the Purgatory. This pilgrim, whose name appears in the Archbishop's Register for 1411 as Lord Laurence Rathold of Postoth in the Kingdom of Hungary, related his experience afterwards in Dublin to one James Yonge, who wrote the account with suitable embellishments. On the same occasion in 1411, an Italian pilgrim, Antonio Mannini, a merchant from Florence, went to Lough Derg. His account of the Purgatory was written up for him, on his return to Florence, by his brother Silvestro Mannini. The translation which follows of the beginning of Mannini's account shows that by the early fifteenth century, stories were current of St Patrick's association with the Cave. The account also illustrates the atmosphere of the pilgrimage, a climate of suspense better known to us in the 'Gothick' romances of several centuries later:

The Purgatory lies in a lake among high mountains which is like a well, ten miles in circumference, in which there are thirty-four islands great and small. We reached the island in that lake on which the Priory stands in safety on Thursday the 4th of November [1411], which island is a mile measured by water from the island of the Purgatory and the said island of the Purgatory is 129 paces long and 30 paces wide and is in the very centre of the said lake. That day, as soon as I arrived, I confessed myself to the Prior of the said Priory and began the usual fast on bread and water as observed by others, according to their desire to do so and the rule of the pilgrimage. I wished to fast for more days, but the Prior urging that it was winter and very cold, would not allow me to fast for more than three consecutive days.

On Saturday the 7th November, 1411, preparing to enter the Purgatory that day, though the Prior was very unwilling, I rose before dawn, and when he had confessed me he said the Mass of our Lord Jesus Christ for me, and then gave me Communion; and after that I heard another Mass of the Annunciation of Our Lady, and then I beseeched the Prior to send me to the Purgatory. When he at last consented with great trouble and difficulty, the canon who said the Mass of Our Lady for me, whose name is Brother John, and who is one of the canons of the said Priory, was commanded to take me to the island of the Purgatory, and put me into it. The said canon put me in a little boat, which was like a piece of roughly hewn hollow tree-trunk, and four persons could hardly find room in it. The Prior accompanied me as far as the water, and put me into the boat himself, first kissing me and giving me his blessing. You must note that I was barefoot and bareheaded, and was wearing a riding tunic and a doublet over my shirt. Then the canon, who sat facing me with his back to the island, began to row with two small oars, and I sat facing him, with my face to the island of the Purgatory.

The weather was still and fine, and it was calm. When we were within half a bow-shot of the said island of the Purgatory I saw a bird blacker than coal take flight: it had not a single plume or feather on its back, save only four or five on each wing, and it was shaped like a heron, but rather larger. When I saw it I thought it a great marvel, and I began to tremble, and my heart beat fast with fear, and my hair stood straight up on end so that I could scarcely smooth it down with my hands and make it lie flat. The canon knew quite well what it was, for he began to make the sign of the cross, crossing himself four or five times. I asked him what it meant, and what this bird might be and the reason of the great fear which had come upon me.

But he answered, trying to put me off, as if he did not wish to tell me, saying (in Latin) *Nothing! it is nothing! do not ask questions! do not ask questions!* and bidding me be of good cheer, and trust in God, and commend myself to him. This made me the more suspicious, and I instantly and piteously besought him in God's name to tell me fully what this might be. Thereupon he replied that since I asked him in the Lord's name, and in such a manner, he could not refuse, and he began as follows:

'At the time when our Lord showed St Patrick this Purgatory, after him, and one of his disciples called St Nicholas, many went in, and most of them perished and came forth no more and were never heard of again. St Patrick marvelled greatly at this, and devoutly prayed to God with constant prayer and discipline, until he saw by the Holy Spirit that it was because of a wicked demon called Corna, who by his many and various temptations caused all the people to perish. Then St Patrick made a special prayer to God, beseeching Him to destroy the power of this demon, and God heard his prayer, and appeared to him in visible form in this place on the island, and said, "I have bound him in this shape and he shall never again have power to harm any man, and he shall retain this shape until the Day of Judgment, and he shall not have power to abide anywhere but on a stone or a withered tree, and when any Christian comes to this island he shall go forth therefrom and abide on some other island, but he shall not be able to leave the lake."'

Then the canon added that when the accursed bird Corna blows the horn with his beak, like a man, it is a sign of perdition for him who is about to enter the Purgatory. But, God be praised, he did not blow the horn for me, and I heard nothing. If I marvelled, marvel likewise when you hear these words, for to this hour my heart beats when I think of it.

Mannini's graphic description of the Cave itself is of interest and follows in translation. He refrained from giving details of Purgatory, and he was logical enough to question whether his experience was, in fact, a sort of ecstatic dream or an actual physical voyage into the world beyond the grave. This very attitude imparts a ring of truth to his pilgrim's description of the Cave:

The place is three feet wide, nine feet long and high enough for a man to kneel but not to stand upright. It is exactly like a sepulchre, for it is vaulted overhead and lies towards the south, that is, there is a niche about three feet long in the direction of the Chapel, in which the Prior had told me to remain and wait, saying my prayers the while. When I reached it, I remained on my knees in prayer, with the cross in my hand as the Prior had bidden me. I said the Seven Penitential Psalms and the Litanies and then a *Salve Regina* and fifteen *Ave Marias* in honour of the fifteen joys of the Blessed Virgin Mary, and I remember that with great lamentation and most bitter tears I turned to her with all my soul, calling upon her by name and beseeching her to intercede for me with her beloved Son that He might aid me in the salvation of my soul. And as I was praying thus, I fell asleep, and whether my soul was rapt in ecstasy out of my body or whether indeed I journeyed in my actual body, and in what way, I cannot tell you. What I saw and what was shown to me, and what I did, I may not write in a letter, nor can I utter it save in confession, but if ever it pleases God that we should meet again I will tell you all things in due order.

The canon, sent by the Prior, returned at night, and opened the door of the Purgatory and entered. He says he found me senseless and breathless with my head resting upon the cross which I held in my right hand. He says he passed his hands over my face and arms and hands and legs and feet and nearly all my body, and found all colder than ice, so that he doubted whether I was alive. He seized my left arm and shook me violently, and I awoke. I was fearful of danger, as one who is awakened suddenly in terror. He said 'Arise! arise! come to the Prior, for he will not have you stay here any longer.' I, rejoicing at the grace of God, followed him out of the Purgatory. He led me back to the chapel with great delight and joy, making me kneel before the altar, and bidding me render thanks to God with all my heart, which I did. Then he took the cross out of my hand, and stripped the white garment from me. I put on my own clothes. When I was dressed the canon put an ancient Psalter before me on the altar, and bade me open it and read a verse of a psalm. I did so, and chanced upon this verse: *For thy mercy towards me is great, and thou hast delivered my soul from the nethermost Hell.* The canon hearing it recited the Te Deum. Note well, Corso, how much I am beholden to God.

Then the canon took me back in the same boat to the island of the Priory. The Prior and others stood on the shore watching for my return, and when I had landed from the boat they all kissed me, and, rejoicing over me, the Prior led me to the chapel where he had given me Communion in the morning, and said the Te Deum.

I judge that I was five hours in the Purgatory. It is usual to remain there for a day – that is, twenty-four hours, but in such cold weather the Prior would not suffer me to remain longer. I think that place – that is, the whole of the lake, is the coldest country in which I have ever been. The mountains of Brigha are not cold in winter compared to that place. I wonder now how I endured it so long almost naked. Be certain, Corso, it would have been impossible, save by the grace and mercy of God.

The bearer of this will tell you how I came out marked, for I showed him so that he could tell you. Perhaps I shall bear the mark for ever. God's will be done. And so I will end, advising every man to keep himself carefully from vice and sin, for God is Truth and absolute Justice.

Caxton, in his translation of *The Mirrour of the World* of 1480, added to the article on St Patrick's Purgatory observations which he himself had gleaned from a canon of Waterford, to whom he had spoken in person. This cleric claimed to have been into the Cave five or six times and to have suffered no strange experience whatsoever, although he reported that other men had had marvellous dreams when they slept there. Jean de Banste, thrice Burgomaster of Bruges, also told Caxton that he had been in the Cave without seeing anything strange.

It seems that Caxton's informants were not the only persons at the time to doubt that the Cave had any supernatural association. The *Annals of Ulster* for 1497 report that in that year the cave of the Purgatory of St Patrick on Loch Derg was 'broken' by the Guardian of Donegal with representatives of the Bishop and by authorization of the Pope, 'it being understood ... that this was not the Purgatory Patrick got from God', although it was the place that everyone had visited.

According to the Bollandists, who used as their source a codex in Brussels, Pope Alexander VI ordered the Cave to be closed in 1494, following a report he received from a Dutch Augustinian canon from Eymstadt who had been there on a pilgrimage. The Dutch cleric asserted that he had first been required to go to the Bishop of Clogher for a licence to go into the Purgatory. The Bishop demanded a sum of money for the favour, which the Dutchman refused on the grounds of his own poverty, telling the Bishop that even if he had the amount, he would not dare to give it on account of the taint of simony. (This bishop must have been Edmund Courcy, Bishop of Clogher from 1485 until 1494, when he became Bishop of Ross and the see of Clogher remained vacant for eight years.) The Bishop eventually gave the licence without payment, and the Dutch Augustinian went on to the local chieftain whom he referred to as 'the Prince of that territory'. The chieftain also demanded money, and only admitted the pilgrim with difficulty when he realized that, this poor canon having no money, he could not get any out of him. Finally, the canon was able to present his permits from the Bishop and the Prince to the Prior of Lough Derg. Like the others, the Prior demanded a fee, and again the pilgrim had to insist on his poverty, and also plead that to pay would be to commit simony. When, at last, the canon overcame the Prior and gained admittance to the Cave, he waited in its depths prayerfully for an experience of Purgatory. He heard and saw nothing, nor did he suffer any discomfort. Convinced, then, that the local inhabitants were telling strangers that their sins could be purged in the Cave in order to extract money from them, the canon determined to prevent the innocent and ignorant from being so beguiled in the future. He made his way to Rome, where he managed to get his complaint before the Pope, who conceded the request and ordered the closure of the Cave. Perhaps if the canon of Eymstadt had followed the custom of fasting for fifteen days, and had been subjected to lying corpse-like in a coffin for his own Requiem Mass, he might at least have enjoyed a dream of Purgatory, or witnessed some hallucinatory apparitions.

After the destruction of the Cave on Saints' Island the centre of pilgrimage was transferred to Station Island, where a smaller cave was presented as 'the Purgatory'. Many who visited it seem to have been unaware that this was not the cave of medieval fame.

By 1517, when Francesco Chiericati, the Papal Nuncio accredited to King Henry VIII, visited Lough Derg, it seems that a new ritual had been established for the pilgrims. His account says nothing of licences or permits which, apparently, had been abolished. Chiericati's description of his visit is given in a letter he wrote to Isabella d'Este, which appears in translation in her biography by Cartwright.

> We reached the banks of a lake which is four miles round and has a rocky island in the centre, twenty steps long by sixteen wide, which is called the Purgatory of St Patrick and is inhabited by three Canons. By sounding a horn and waving a white handkerchief on the end of a pole, we summoned one of the Canon's two servants, who rowed us one by one across the lake in a rude bark made of a hollow beech-trunk, for which we paid a penny each. Here we landed and found a little Oratory, with a hut and tables for the canons. In front of the church-door are the three cabins of St Bridget, St Patrick and St Columba. Behind, towards the East, is the Well of St Patrick, a cave in which the Saint is said to have slept. It holds twelve people and has an iron door; but I did not go inside fearing to see terrible things. So I remained outside standing three steps from the door and the Canons went in with two pine torches. I looked at the roof which is rock like a millstone, and when you strike it you hear an echo and this has given rise to the fables we hear about St Patrick's Well.

Two of my companions entered the cave with five other pilgrims, but I think my penance was worse than theirs, as I had to await their return nearly ten days, and during that time I consumed the greater part of the victuals we had brought with us.

On the day of your arrival you make your will if you have anything to leave. Then you confess and fast on bread and water for nine days and visit the three cabins every hour, saying any number of prayers. And you have to stand in the Lake, some up to the knees, others halfway up their bodies and some up to their necks. At the end of nine days you hear Mass, communicate, and are blessed and signed with holy water and go with the cross before you to the gate of St Patrick's Well. Then you go inside and the door is closed, and not opened until the next day, as you have to stay there twenty-four hours. The rock is pierced on one side and a dish with food is put in through this hole by one of the Canons, who stands there and exhorts the pilgrims to be constant and not to be overcome by the temptations of the Devil, for it is said that all manner of horrible visions appear to them and many come out idiots or madmen, because they have yielded to temptation. Of those who entered the cave when I was present, two saw such fearful things that one went out of his mind and when he was questioned, declared that he had been beaten violently, but he did not know by whom. Another had seen beautiful women, who had invited him to eat with them, and offered him fruit and food of all sorts, and these were almost vanquished. The others saw and felt nothing but great cold, hunger and weakness and came out half-dead the next day...

The cold-water punishment seen administered to the souls in Purgatory had, it seems, been transformed at the new site into cold-water immersion for the pilgrim penitents.

Scepticism about the Purgatory which had begun in Caxton's time, and which resulted in the demolition of the Saints' Island cave and the reduction of the pilgrimage to Station Island to a spiritual rather than a supernatural experience, is echoed in the opinion of the Jesuit Father Edmund Campion. Campion, the Renaissance man, was writing in 1570 when the informed inhabitants of Europe knew that Ireland was not the extremity of the world, and that another earthly continent lay beyond the western ocean. Campion admitted that it might please God, on certain occasions, to reveal miraculously to a human creature a vision of eternal joy or eternal pain, but he firmly dismissed as ignorant superstition any pretension of the Lough Derg cave to supernatural quality.

Campion's opinion was promulgated by Holinshed in his *Chronicles of England, Scotland and Ireland*, 1578, and by the Jesuit Richard Stanihurst in his *Vita Patricii*, a life of St Patrick printed at Antwerp in 1587. Stanihurst asserted that those who had locked themselves in St

Patrick's Purgatory in his time had experienced no terrors, indeed nothing more than, occasionally, a deep sleep. This, of course, implies that the cave was still open. Stanihurst continued with a further explanation of the reputation of the Purgatory. '... in the first seed-time of religion, the period when miracles are far more frequent, I believe it is true that many horrible and terrible shapes to the sight were wont to appear before the eyes of penitents'.

One of the compilers of the *Annals of the Four Masters*, Michael O'Clery, recorded, about 1600, the instructions given to pilgrim penitents at the Purgatory. The round of penance had become far more complicated than that described by Chiericati eighty years earlier. The exercise still took ten days. For nine days the penitent made complicated perambulations around the island, the directions being described with intricate care; he recited prayers and kissed certain stones, crosses and the chapel door. For all this time the penitent observed a fast of but one meal of bread and water a day. Then he spent twenty-four hours in one of two caves, abstaining from all food and drink. Finally the penitent immersed himself three times in the water at a place called St Patrick's Pool.

An official report of 1603 stated that the Priory of Lough Derg 'commonly called St Patrick's Purgatory' was 'much in decay and for many years past has been totally abandoned and dissolved'.

Devotion to St Patrick, however, survived, and with it the tradition that he had been vouchsafed a vision of Purgatory. The antiphon at the Magnificat for the Office of St Patrick in an early seventeenth-century Paris edition was 'Magni patris sunt miranda merita Patricii, cui Dominus ostendit locum Purgatorii, quo viventes se expurgent delinquentes filii,' and the fourth verse of the hymn sung at the Hours was:

Hic est Doctor benevolus
Hibernicorum Apostolus
Cui loca Purgatoria
Ostendit Dei gratia.

which may be translated as:

He is the benevolent teacher,
The Apostle of the Irish,
To whom the place Purgatory
Was revealed by God's grace.

Nor did popular interest in the islands on Lough Derg abate, even though the Priory had been dissolved and pilgrimages had ceased for many years. In the reign of King Charles I the religious climate seemed slightly more relaxed, and intolerance towards the Roman Catholics in Ireland on the part of the authorities was less harsh. In 1631 the Roman Catholic Primate, Hugh O'Reilly, was able to write to Rome about St Patrick's Purgatory: 'The storm of persecution made this Purgatory inaccessible for many years back to the great grief of the Irish. But now ... things being changed a little for the better it is distinguished by innumerable crowds of pilgrims ...'. The Archbishop made known to the Vatican authorities his concern that spiritual direction be provided for the pilgrims, and explained that for this reason he had appointed some Franciscans to assume that task, they being the only Regulars available and well fitted for the purpose. Consequently the Archbishop and the deputy Vicar Apostolic of Clogher petitioned Rome to grant papal approval.

It seems that Archbishop O'Reilly was optimistic in his opinion that things had changed for the better. Within months of his letter to Rome the Privy Council ordered the Purgatory to be seized 'unto His Majesty's use'. For that purpose the Privy Council sent Sir William Stuart and others to Lough Derg. Sir William reached the island called St Patrick's Purgatory where, he reported to the Privy Council, he found '431 persons doing such fooleries as is not to be imagined could be done among Christians'.

Contemporary accounts of the practices of the pilgrims in the seventeenth century describe the 'fooleries' that scandalized Sir William. From the Roman Catholic side, there is an account in Father John Lynch's *Life of Francis Kirwan, Bishop of Killala*, printed in Germany in 1669. According to this account, the pilgrim to St Patrick's Purgatory fasted for nine days, taking no food save a little bread, and water from the lake. On one of the nine days the pilgrim was shut up in the darkness of a cavern, taking no food at all and only enough water to moisten the throat. Thrice a day, at morning, noon and evening, the pilgrim went on bended knees over paths strewn with small sharp stones. The penitent also went a considerable distance into the water of the lake either standing or on his knees. The rest of the time was devoted to reciting prayers and listening to homilies. At night the pilgrim rested on a bed of straw without a pillow. Father Lynch had probably heard criticisms of the pilgrimage, for he added '... nor in this sacred place is there to be seen or heard anything scurrilous or laughable'.

A detailed Protestant description of the practices is furnished in an account written in 1647 by the Protestant Bishop of Clogher. Bishop Jones wrote without bias, and had informed himself from the most exact Roman Catholic sources he could find. The pilgrims, according to Bishop Jones' account, were first examined and admitted. They entered the church barefoot and, kneeling before the altar, recited a Paternoster, an Ave and the Credo; then they made seven circuits inside the church, kissing the door of the church when they left to make seven more circuits in the churchyard, and to walk barefoot or go on their knees seven times around each of the cells called the 'Beds of the Saints'. Next they went to the water, to the stone reputed to be the one on which Patrick knelt in prayer, and made three circuits of it, reciting five Paternosters, five Aves and the Credo. Then they went to a stone covered with water which was called 'Lackevanny', the one said to bear the impression of Patrick's feet. Here they recited prayers and rested their tired, bruised and cut feet under water on the stone. This stone was reputed to have a curative quality, and the pilgrims asserted that in less than fifteen minutes resting on it while saying the Paternoster and the Apostles' Creed, they became entirely refreshed and ready to go on.

Returning to the church, the pilgrims recited a rote of prayers called the Lady's Psalter. This whole procedure was repeated thrice daily, at morning, noon and night for seven days. On the eighth day all the prayers and circuits were doubled in number. During the nine days of the pilgrimage the penitents took food only once each twenty-four hours, and then only bread or oatmeal and water. At night they slept on straw without a pillow, for four nights in one of the cottages, for four nights in the open on the Saints' Beds. After confession on the

evening of the eighth day they prepared to spend the ninth in the Cave. In imitation of the old custom, the priest treated them to a homily in which he enjoined them not to proceed with their intention of entering the Cave, warning them that two companies of penitents had been lost and that it was ordained that one more company would be lost there and not return. The procession to the Cave, with the banner of the Cross at its head, was made with solemn funereal pomp, the pilgrims groaning, sighing and weeping. The pilgrims were then shut in the Cave, without food for twenty-four hours and observing total silence. On emerging, the pilgrims went down to the lake where they immersed themselves totally in its waters, intending by this bath of repentance to symbolize their rebirth as soldiers of Christ after being purged of their sins. Before leaving they paid a last visit to the church.

Sir William Stuart on the occasion of his visit, disgusted by all he saw, had the pilgrims shipped to the shore, and, not being able to find the Franciscans who had been warned of his arrival and fled, he informed the servants of McGrath – the owner of the boat and the temporal landlord – that the island was not to be frequented until the King's wishes concerning the place should be further known. This McGrath was a James McGrath, a descendant of the chiefs long associated with the Purgatory and hereditary custodians (*erenaghs*) of the ecclesiastical site. Following Sir William's visit the Lord Chancellor required James McGrath to enter into a bond for one thousand pounds that he would '...pull down and utterly demolish that monster of fame called Saint Patrick's Purgatory, with Saint Patrick's Bed and all the vaults, cells and other houses and buildings and to have all the other superstitious stones and materials cast into the Lough and that he should suffer the superstitious Chapel in the Island to be pulled down to the ground and no boat to be there nor pilgrimage used nor frequented ...'.

To be sure that the demolition was effected, the Lords Justices and Privy Council sent an order in 1632 to the Protestant Bishop of Clogher, the High Sheriff of the County of Donegal and three other gentlemen requiring them 'by or before the third day of December next to cause the Chapel and all the Irish houses in that Island called St Patrick's Purgatory, all the buildings, pavements, walls, works, foundations, Circles, Caves, Cells and Vaults thereof of lime or stone or otherwise to be broken down, defaced and utterly demolished and that also called St Patrick's Bed, as also that rock or stone standing in the water there having a clift in it which, as is vainly said, St Patrick made kneeling at his prayers: And also that stone covered there with water which hath the point of a man's foot and which, as the seduced people do believe, St Patrick made with standing thereon ...'.

Clearly the legend had grown apace, and St Patrick's physical association with the place was attested by knee-holes and footprints. The departure of the Augustinians and decades of abandonment had only served to increase interest in the Purgatory. The strength of its popular attraction did not escape the Privy Council, who admitted in their Order that '... the seduced people will secretly find opportunity to resort hither and so by stealth continue their superstitious abuses, while the place standeth...'

The demolition duly took place in October. The High Sheriff of County Donegal and the other gentlemen charged with the task claimed that they were unable to find any labourers willing to undertake the task. On the day arranged for those commissioned to meet at Lough Derg, the High Sheriff of County Donegal did not turn up, and the High Sheriff of County Fermanagh, who came with one servant, was unwilling to cross to the Island. Undaunted, the Protestant Bishop of Clogher, who had brought twenty armed men and the necessary tools, went with them over to the Island, and, as he reported to the Protestant Primate, they diligently pulled down the Chapel and the Irish houses and broke down the Circles and Saints' Beds. Bishop Spottiswoode found no secret passage or even any depth to the place called the Cave, which he described as 'a poor beggarly hole, made with some stones, laid together with men's hands without any great art and after covered with earth such as husbandmen make to keep a few hogs from the rain'.

King Charles I's consort, the French Henrietta Maria, a Roman Catholic, was asked to intercede with the authorities to allow pilgrimages to continue. Six years after the demolition, in 1638, she wrote in French to Wentworth, the Lord Deputy of Ireland, telling him that he would do her a great pleasure if he would allow the devotion not to be abolished, and assuring him that the people would avail themselves of the privilege modestly. Wentworth replied politely and very diplomatically to the Queen that, as the site had been absolutely destroyed and was in the middle of the Scottish Plantations, it would be unwise to restore it, much as he would have liked to please the Queen by doing so, and he recommended that the Queen be patient and wait for a more opportune moment in the future in which to effect her satisfaction in the matter.

The next decade brought reversals to the monarchy, and the Queen had far more pressing problems to face than the question of the restoration of St Patrick's Purgatory. For the Irish people, however, the forbidden became only more desired. For the Roman Catholic hierarchy the question of the Purgatory became a point of honour, another battle to be won against the heretics. Ireland became embroiled in the Civil War, and was plunged into a complicated state of strife between the factions because of the conflicting loyalties which obtained there. Nevertheless, in the midst of his delicate mission to Ireland during the war, the Papal Nuncio, Archbishop Rinuccini, found time to worry about the fate of the Purgatory. In 1648 Rinuccini wrote to Pope Innocent X that he hoped O'Neill's forces would be able to free St Patrick's Purgatory from the hands of the heretics. The Nuncio considered the feat of wresting the holy place from the Protestants was equal to 'any of the most glorious of Apostolic missions' that he had fulfilled, but he had to report to the Pope that it had not been possible to execute his plan to recover the Purgatory due to lack of funds for the expedition.

It is clear that Rinuccini had been informed that Patrick himself had been at Lough Derg. As he wrote in his letter to the Pope: 'It is known that the Saint chose this place for his devotions in retirement and the revelations which it pleased God to communicate to him have been believed and perhaps proved by posterity.' The legend was becoming more deeply entrenched, and the Purgatory only more hallowed by the objections made to it by the English authorities.

It seems that even the destruction of the chapel, the cave and the places of veneration at Lough Derg, and the prohibition against pilgrimages, did not effectively stop penitents from going there. The island remained in a desolate, ruinous state. A party of Protestants who visited it in 1701 found only heaps of stones and an improvised altar. Yet in 1704, a little more than seventy years after the demolition, it was found necessary for Parliament to pass an Act prohibiting pilgrimages, and mentioning specifically the pilgrimage to Lough Derg. That the Purgatory was once again then frequented by pilgrims is clearly implied by the words of the Act: '... the superstitions of Popery are greatly increased and upheld by the pretended sanctity of places especially a place called St Patrick's Purgatory in the County of Donegal, and of Wells, to which Pilgrimages are made by vast numbers at certain seasons ...'. The Act also speaks of 'the riotous and unlawful assembling together of many thousands of Papists to the said Wells and other places'. The Act made all such meetings and assemblies illegal, and required the sheriffs, justices of the peace and magistrates to be diligent in apprehending and punishing the persons who participated. A fine of ten shillings was prescribed for any person found meeting or assembling at St Patrick's

Purgatory. The money paid in fines was to be divided equally between the informer whose witness caused the offender to be convicted, and the poor of the parish. Any offender unwilling or unable to pay the fine was to be publicly whipped.

A few years after the Act was passed, the Roman Catholic Bishop of Clogher made a surreptitious visit to the Purgatory disguised as a Dublin tradesman. Fear of the penalties consequent on the Act had not deterred pilgrims. In his diocesan report to Rome in 1714, the Bishop stated that each year from the beginning of June to the end of August, thousands of men and women of every age and condition and from even the remotest parts of Ireland came to make a nine-day fast and penitential rounds on the island of St Patrick's Purgatory. Curiously, Bishop McMahon wrote of 'a subterraneous pit' in which the penitents spent the twenty-four hours of the ninth day, recalling the pit or cavern of the medieval accounts, but at variance with the accounts of seventeenth-century visitors, who sought for an underground place but found no trace of any.

An account of 1727 describes the Cave as being 22 feet in length but only 2 foot 1 inch wide and 3 feet high, little or none of it underground, with one spike-hole to let in air, and a bend 6 feet from the far end. It appears that this Cave must have been constructed since 1701, when visitors had found only heaps of stones.

The Bishop opined that it must be due to a special favour of Divine Providence and to the merits of St Patrick that despite the climate of persecution then prevailing, the bitter Scottish Calvinists settled in the neighbourhood of Lough Derg were doing little or nothing to hinder the pilgrimages, and the pious penitential activities continued.

Bishop McMahon found the grim austerity of the pilgrimage, the continual celebration of Masses from dawn until noon, and the contrition of the pilgrims who frequently interrupted the preacher with their 'copious tears, sobs, lamentations, and other marks of penance', all very uplifting. He mentioned that on the occasion of his own visit, an English Protestant, who had come there out of curiosity, was so moved to compunction by the penitents that he abjured heresy on the spot and embraced the Roman Catholic faith.

Bishop McMahon's only objection to the practices he saw was that the Requiem Mass was celebrated for those about to enter the Cave. He found this canonically improper; but when he voiced his objections, the Franciscans claimed the authority of immemorial custom and stated that St Patrick himself had originated the tradition. Other learned ecclesiastics assured the Bishop that this was so, and, perplexed, he asked Rome to instruct him on the matter. In consequence, the scholarly Pope Benedict XIII caused research to be undertaken on the history of the Purgatory. He concluded from this that there was no evidence that St Patrick had founded the Purgatory, and ended on a diplomatic-devotional note by quoting St Pietro Callense, that the Blessed Virgin was the true pit or well ('puteus') from which forgiveness for sins could be drawn, and temptations healed.

The old customs, nevertheless, were not abandoned. In a Latin guide to St Patrick's Purgatory published at Louvain in 1735, the author, an Irish Dominican priest, explained that the pilgrims prepared themselves for death and burial, and that a Requiem Mass was said for them before they entered the Cave. This guidebook explains, also, that as the number of pilgrims was usually so great that they could not all enter the old cave, another cave had been built of stones beside the chapel to accommodate them, and that on occasions when both caves were full, those who could not enter them made their twenty-four-hour vigil of silence, fasting and prayer in the chapel. The author of the guidebook, Father Dominic Brullaughan, believed that St Patrick himself had had the original deep and terrible Cave divinely shown to him on Saints' Island, the larger island, and that he had built the monastery there. Father Brullaughan explained that at some later date, but long since, the Augustinians canons, because the presence of the pilgrims was a nuisance to them, and because they deemed it a more suitable place for mortification, prayer and penance, had transferred the place of pilgrimage to the smaller island.

By 1786, reconstruction had resulted in the island having two chapels and fifteen thatched houses to accommodate the clergy and penitents during the pilgrimages. There were seven heaps of rough stones, each encircled by an outer row of stones and surmounted by a cross. The 'Cave' was described then as a low, narrow vault capable of accommodating about twelve persons. An old man living in the 1820s also remembered the Cave as such from his pilgrimage made about 1780, but found on his return in 1819 that it had vanished and been replaced by a commodious chapel dedicated to St Patrick. He was told that the Prior had caused the earlier Cave to be demolished about 1790 because too many pilgrims attempted to crowd into it.

13 A processional Station on Station Island, Lough Derg, where pilgrims undertake one of Christendom's most rigorous and ascetic devotional exercises. Behind can be seen the basilica and residential buildings

14 A processional Station near the shore on Station Island, Lough Derg, where pilgrims kneel, recite penitential prayers silently and renounce the world, the flesh and the devil with outstretched arms

15 Some of the most devout pilgrims to Croaghpatrick welcome the painful mortification of climbing the steep mountain without shoes

16 St Patrick's Well at Cloghan Head, near Kilteel, Co. Down, one of the many wells throughout the country long traditionally associated with St Patrick

The antiquarian John O'Donovan visited both Saints' Island and Station Island in the late autumn of 1835. On the former, which he referred to as St Daveog's Island, he noticed the groundworks of a number of ruins. It appeared to O'Donovan that when the place of pilgrimage was removed from Saints' Island to the smaller island, some of the venerated stones were moved there to remake the crosses and Saints' Beds. O'Donovan was informed that each year during the *p. 127* Station season, between 1 June and 15 August, as many as seven thousand persons made the arduous pilgrimage.

On Saints' Island, only traces of stone walls with rectangular enclosures now remain. The little Station Island, on the other hand, *plates 13, 14* is almost completely covered with buildings, the result of the activities of a succession of priors since the Prior Father O'Doherty built a chapel, St Mary's, on the island in 1762, when the ban on pilgrimages was on the statute books. The eighteenth-century chapel was replaced in 1870 by the modest St Mary's Church still in use today. In front of it are four two-storey houses of Georgian style. There is a three-storey hospice for pilgrims built in 1880–82, an unpretentious building now disimproved by alterations. A statue of the Virgin sculpted in Dublin in 1882 stands in front of this hospice, along with two Italian statues representing St Patrick and St Joseph, purchased in Carrara in 1891 by the Bishop of Clogher. The newer hospice, an unprepossessing three-storey building which accommodates 220 cubicles, was designed by the architect William A. Scott in 1912. Scott also designed in 1921 the basilica dedicated to St Patrick.

In this massive centrally-planned church, which was begun in 1924 and built in phases after Scott's death by T. J. Cullen, the architect expressed Byzantine elements within an Irish-Romansque Revival framework. The plan of St Patrick's is octagonal with short cruciform arms; circular towers flank the entrance.

Between St Patrick's and St Mary's are the Saints' Beds, circular dry-stone constructions, none more than 3 feet in height and all but one measuring between 10 and 12 feet in diameter; a larger one, St Molaise's Bed, is 16 feet in diameter. The shaft of a twelfth-century cross, called St Patrick's Cross, is believed to have been brought to Station Island from its original home on Saints' Island.

17 These nuns are among the fifty thousand pilgrims who make the arduous ascent of Croaghpatrick on the annual pilgrimage. Some begin the climb on the Saturday night and keep vigil on the summit until the Oratory is open for the celebration of the first of the Sunday Masses at 5 a.m.

Today the mystical and spiritual aspects of the penitential exercise are stressed. The sensational aspects once associated with the pilgrimage to St Patrick's Purgatory are rarely mentioned save by historians. The element of instilling fear has vanished from the exhortations of the priests to those who still come from all parts of Ireland, and from many countries abroad, as pilgrims to the place which a writer in the *Tablet* has called 'the Mecca of the Gaelic people'. This comparison recalls a verse of an old Irish hymn to Lough Derg composed by Tuileagna mac Torna:

Ar Loch Dearg is deánta dhúinn
ni sgéal leis nach bearthair buaidh
biaidh ar séala deas 'n-a dheoidh
Réalda an eoil theas agus thuaidh.

It has been rendered in English as:

To Lough Derg I must speed,
The guiding-star of East and West.
The mark it will leave on me will be a fair one.
Nothing grander could befall me.

Although the duration of the pilgrimage has been reduced to three days, it is still a rigorous spiritual and physical exercise. The short crossing from the shore to Station Island separates the pilgrim from the bustle and the materialism of a frantic consumer society. The unworldly austerity of the pilgrimage has been retained; fasting, suffering, self-denial, prayer, vigil, renunciation and repentance are the essence of the unique penitential experience leading to reconciliation.

The ascetic discipline of the pilgrimage now in vigour is best illustrated by citing verbatim the leaflet of Regulations regarding admission to Lough Derg published with the approval of the Bishop of Clogher in 1974.

Saint Patrick's Purgatory

Lough Derg, County Donegal

'Unless you repent you will all perish' (Luke 13:3)

ADMISSION

(a) No one under 14 years of age is admitted to the Island.
(b) Cameras, radios and rugs are not allowed.

THE FAST

The pilgrim observes *a complete fast from all food and drink* (plain water excepted) from midnight prior to arriving on Lough Derg. The fast continues for three full days during which one Lough Derg meal a day is allowed.

The first meal is taken when the pilgrim has made at least one Station on the Island, the second may be taken at any time in the afternoon of the second day, and the third as soon as the pilgrim leaves Lough Derg.

On the third day the meal should be similar to those taken on the Island and the pilgrim may drink, as often as he chooses, any of the minerals approved. A list of these minerals may be seen in the hospices. The fast ends at midnight of the third day.

THE VIGIL

The vigil is the chief penitential exercise of the Pilgrimage and means depriving oneself of sleep, completely and continuously, for 24 hours. It begins at 10.00 p.m. on the first day and ends after Benediction on the second day. At that time the pilgrim retires to bed.

THE STATIONS

As soon as he arrives on the Island the pilgrim begins his first Stations and completes three Stations before 9.30 p.m.

A Station is fully described overleaf.

The prayers of four Stations are said aloud in common in the Basilica during the night of the Vigil. Between these Stations pilgrims may leave the Basilica, use the night shelter, and walk around the immediate vicinity of the Basilica only.

A further Station is made later in the morning when the pilgrim has been to Confession and the final one on the third day after the Papal Blessing.

HOW TO MAKE A STATION

Note: When making a Station always turn to the right and say the prayers silently.

Begin the Station with a visit to the Blessed Sacrament in *St Patrick's Basilica.*

Then go to *St Patrick's Cross,* near the Basilica; kneel, and say one Our Father, one Hail Mary and one Creed.

Go to *St Brigid's Cross,* on the outside wall of the Basilica; kneel, and say three Our Fathers, three Hail Marys and One Creed. Stand with your back to the Cross and renounce three times with your outstretched arms the World, the Flesh and the Devil.

Make four rounds of *the Basilica* while saying seven decades of the Rosary and one Creed at the end.

Go to the penitential cell or 'bed' called *St Brigid's Bed,* i.e. the one farthest from the Basilica, but take care to join the queue of pilgrims (if there is a queue) before going to the Bed.

At the Bed (a) walk three times round the outside, by your right hand, while saying three Our Fathers, three Hail Marys and one Creed;

(b) kneel at the entrance to the Bed and repeat these prayers;

(c) walk three times round the inside and say these prayers again;

(d) kneel at the Cross in the centre and say these prayers for the fourth time.

Do the same again at

St Brendan's Bed
St Catherine's Bed
St Columba's Bed

Make six rounds of the outside of *the large Penitential Bed* (which comprises St Patrick's Bed and that of Sts Davog and Molaise) while saying six Our Father, six Hail Marys and one Creed.

Kneel at the entrance to *St Patrick's Bed* (nearer the men's hospice) and say three Our Fathers, three Hail Marys and one Creed. Walk three times around the inside while repeating these prayers. Kneel at the Cross in the centre and say them again.

Kneel at the entrance to *the Bed of Sts Davog and Molaise* (nearer the water's edge) and say three Our Fathers, three Hail Marys and one Creed. Walk three times round the inside while repeating these prayers. Kneel at the Cross in the centre and say them again.

Go to *the water's edge;* stand, and say five Our Fathers, five Hail Marys and One Creed. Kneel and repeat these prayers.

Return to *St Patrick's Cross;* kneel, and say one Our Father, one Hail Mary and one Creed.

Conclude the Station in *the Basilica* by saying five Our Fathers, five Hail Marys and one Creed for the Pope's intentions.

The Apostles' Creed

I believe in God, the Father Almighty, Creator of heaven and earth; and in Jesus Christ, his only Son, Our Lord, who was conceived by the Holy Ghost; born of the Virgin Mary; suffered under Pontius Pilate; was crucified, died and was buried; he descended into hell; the third day he rose again from the dead; he ascended into Heaven, sitteth at the right hand of God the Father almighty; from thence he shall come to judge the living and the dead. I believe in the Holy Ghost; the Holy Catholic Church; the communion of Saints; the forgiveness of sins; the resurrection of the body, and life everlasting.

AMEN

ORDER OF EXERCISES

First Day

Arrive, fasting from midnight, register as pilgrim and await boat. Boats are available from 11.00 a.m. until 3.00 p.m. and pilgrims do well to arrive as early as possible.

Afternoon	Begin Stations and complete three by 9.30 p.m.
6.30 p.m.	Holy Mass
9.30 p.m.	Evening Prayer and Benediction of the Blessed Sacrament
10.15–11.15	Holy Hour
11.45 p.m.	Rosary
12.30 a.m.	Fourth Station
2.00 a.m.	Fifth Station
3.30 a.m.	Sixth Station
5.00 a.m.	Seventh Station

Second Day

6.30 a.m.	Morning Prayer, Mass and Instruction Blessing of religious objects
8.30 a.m.	Confession in St Mary's Church After Confession make Eighth Station
12 noon	Stations of the Cross
6.30 p.m.	Holy Mass
9.30 p.m.	Night Prayer and Benediction of the Blessed Sacrament
10.00 p.m.	Retire to bed

Third Day

6.00 a.m.	Bell for rising
6.30 a.m.	Morning Prayer, Mass and Instruction. Papal Blessing after which the final Station is begun

The time of departure of boats is announced each morning after Mass.

VIII
The Cult of St Patrick

Today, fifteen centuries after Patrick's mission to the Irish, his cult is more widespread than it has ever been. His feast day is the occasion of religious and secular celebrations not only in Ireland, where St Patrick's Day is the national holiday of the Republic, but also in many countries abroad.

By far the biggest and most extraordinary manifestation ostensibly in honour of St Patrick now must be the St Patrick's Day parade in New York City, an astounding extravaganza in which a million or more New Yorkers of the most varied ethnic origins express their affection for things Irish. The first St Patrick's Day march in the city took place on 17 March 1762, several years before America declared her independence from Great Britain. On every St Patrick's Day since, there has been a parade. Since its significance was carried on the wings of Irish nationalism, it is not surprising that today the figure of the fifth-century Christian missionary has become obscured by the razamatazz and array of secular emblems associated with a late eighteenth- and nineteenth-century image of Ireland, ranging from the shamrock and the colour green to shillelaghs, wolfhounds and even leprechauns.

It is an extraordinary sight to see one hundred thousand people march down Fifth Avenue, even when there is a bitterly cold wind or occasional snow-flurries, while the police obligingly close off city blocks to traffic for several hours in the busiest part of mid-town Manhattan and marshal one million applauding onlookers behind barricades erected along the route from 44th to 86th Street.

The parade itself has become a stupendous succession of high-stepping honour guards, smartly costumed, baton-twirling, high-booted drum-majorettes, elegant, scarlet-coated horsewomen mounted side-saddle on thoroughbred hunters, children leading Irish wolf-hounds, police bands, military bands, veterans' bands, trade union bands, parochial bands, college bands, high-school bands, bands with exotic names like the Piscataway Superchief Band and the Westhampton Hurricane Marching Band, and bands of ethnic provenance like the bagpipers of the St Columcille United Gaelic Pipe Band from Kearny, New Jersey. In 1981 the young musicians of the Thurles, Co. Tipperary, Silver Band were flown over from Ireland to participate.

New York's Roman Catholic cathedral on Fifth Avenue is dedicated to St Patrick, as is the archdiocese of New York. Six thousand worshippers attend the eight Masses in the cathedral on a Sunday, and each year an estimated three million persons visit the imposing building, completed in 1879; but never is it more thronged or more the centre of attention than for the celebration of the Mass and the parade on St Patrick's Day. After the religious observances the Cardinal Archbishop reviews the parade from its steps, while the Governor of the State of New York, the Mayor of the city and other dignitaries review the marchers from a grandstand farther along the avenue.

The association of St Patrick with the chief emblem sported, the shamrock, appears to have no roots in antiquity. The legend that Patrick explained the mystery of the Holy Trinity to his neophytes with its aid is mentioned in print for the first time as late as the eighteenth century (in the preface entitled 'A Short Treatise on Native Plants especially such as grow spontaneously in the vicinity of Dublin' of Caleb Threlkeld's *Synopsis Stirpium Hibernarum*, published in 1727):

> This plant is worn by the people in their hats on the 17th of March yearly, which is called St Patrick's Day, it being a current tradition that, by this three-leaved grass, he emblematically set forth to them the mystery of the Holy Trinity. However that may be when they wet their *seamar-oge* they often commit excess in liquor ...

There is no satisfactory evidence before the seventeenth century of association of the shamrock with either St Patrick or his feast day. Coins minted at Kilkenny in the latter part of the seventeenth century bear the figure of the Saint in episcopal vestments and holding aloft a large trifoliate plant. Thomas Dinely, an English traveller who made a tour of Ireland in 1681, commented in his *Journal*:

> The 17th day of March yearly is St Patrick's, an immoveable feast when ye Irish of all stations and condicions were [sic] crosses in their hats, some of pins, some of green ribbon, and the vulgar superstitiously wear shamroges, 3-leaved grass, which they likewise eat, they say, to cause a sweet breath.

The question of the antiquity of the shamrock in Patrician lore must, therefore, remain doubtful, although W.H. Grattan Flood has pointed out that a trefoil appears in the ornamentation of the *Books of Kells*, in the ninth-century St Gall antiphony, and in the carved relief of some early Irish Christian stone crosses.

The Shamrock certainly appears to have been eaten by the Irish, but more probably from necessity than to sweeten their breath as Dinely was told. In the preceding century, Edmund Campion wrote in 1571 of 'Shamrotes' which with watercresses and other herbs formed part of the diet in Munster, and Edmund Spenser, writing about ten years after Campion, also alluded to this item of diet.

In the eighteenth century the custom of wearing shamrock gradually replaced the custom of wearing a cross in the hat. A caricature of four gentlemen by Sir Joshua Reynolds in 1751 portrays the Irish gentlemen (Lord Charlemont) with a bunch of shamrock so worn. By the nineteenth century the custom was widespread. The green of the green ribbon mentioned by Dinely in 1681 likewise grew in popularity, so that eventually, in 1797, it was adopted as the colour of the 'nationalist' party in Ireland, and was thus commemorated in a street ballad 'The wearin' of the Green'. Boucicault added verses to this popular song, but the original version ran:

O Paddy dear, an' did ye hear the news that's goin' round?
The shamrock is by law forbid to grow on Irish ground.
No more St Patrick's Day we'll keep, his colour can't be seen,
For there's a cruel law agin the wearin' o' the Green.
I met wid Napper Tandy, and he took me by the hand,
And he said 'How's poor ould Ireland, and how does she stand?'
She's the most disthressful country that iver yet was seen
For they're hangin' men an' women there for the wearin' o' the Green.

Nowhere, surely, can the 'wearin' o' the green' be more in evidence than among the New Yorkers celebrating St Patrick's Day. Chinese restaurants in the city, swathed in green bunting, serve green rice and green noodles and serenade customers with 'I'll Take You Home Again Kathleen', while Italian restaurants, also swathed in green bunting, serve lasagna verde and vino verde; bars offer not only green cocktails but green beer. On the streets, New Yorkers, both black and white, can be seen sporting green boots and green fur coats, and walking dogs wearing bright green bows. While the more conservative citizens may not go beyond a green rosette or a buttonhole of a white carnation dyed green, the fantasy of others runs to green false moustaches and green plastic bowler hats. Youngsters can be seen with green-dyed hair and green shamrocks tattooed or painted on their faces. Inside St Patrick's Cathedral banks of white flowers dyed green are arranged before the altar.

It is not, of course, only in New York City that this display of green is to be seen on 17 March. Cities like Chicago and Boston which welcomed large numbers of Irish immigrants have splendid parades, but so does Washington, the nation's capital. Des Moines, lowa, organized its first St Patrick's Day parade in 1981 followed by a reception at the Civic Centre where Irish stew and Irish coffee were served to the guests. But surely the citizens of San Antonio, Texas, who dye the San Antonio river green on St Patrick's Day must be considered worthy rivals of the New Yorkers who paint a green line down Fifth Avenue.

The boisterous celebration of 17 March was revived in Sydney, Australia, in 1980 with a long march from the Haymarket to the Opera House, where an out-of-doors concert was staged with pipe-bands, Irish folk bands on tabletop trucks, flags, shillelaghs and cheer squads. More soberly, St Patrick's Day as the national day of the Irish State is marked by official receptions in the Irish embassies and diplomatic missions abroad, especially in Rome, where both the Embassy to the Italian State and the Embassy to the Holy See open their doors to official guests and the Irish community. In 1981, the first St Patrick's Day reception in China was given in Peking by the Irish Ambassador.

In Ireland, the national holiday is celebrated throughout the Republic, and also in the six counties of Ulster which are attached to the United Kingdom. There in the North, the Ancient Order of Hibernians stages a traditional demonstration at Feeny, Co. Derry, at which twenty to thirty bands lead contingents from Derry and other parts of the province, and from counties farther afield in the Republic. The principal religious ceremonies in the North are now a Mass celebrated in Irish by the Roman Catholic Primate at Armagh and an ecumenical service at Downpatrick. In Belfast, a large parade which attracts thousands in the Catholic neighbourhood of the Falls Road and Andersonstown has a distinctly nationalist and republican aspect.

In the Republic, the Irish Prime Minister, the *Taoiseach*, and the Lord Mayor of Dublin review the parade of floats as they pass down the capital's broad O'Connell Street. At Longford, over one hundred marching bands participate. At Limerick, as many as forty thousand watch the parade, in which visiting American policemen of the Boston Emerald Society have marched. Ministers of the Government scatter to attend the parades in the provincial cities, among which Cork and Sligo claim the largest attendance, but many small towns and even villages boast parades with bands and floats.

The background for most of this enthusiasm must be seen in the association of the Day and the Irish emblems with Irish nationalist aspirations, and it is interesting to examine the earlier growth of the Saint's cult over the centuries since his death, not only in Ireland but also in Britain and continental Europe.

In Ireland, the most important Patrician relic, revered there for centuries, was the staff used by the Saint, and believed to have been the one used by Christ himself, the pious tradition being that Patrick had received it from a man blessed with miraculous longevity who had received it from Christ when he was on earth (p. 73). Known therefore as the *Baculus Jesu* (in Irish, *Bachall Jesa*), this crozier or pastoral staff, encased in gold inlaid with precious stones, was kept in the church at Armagh up to the time of the Anglo-Norman conquest of Ireland. The annalists record instances of its use, when oaths were sworn on it and peace treaties sealed between warring chiefs. At the end of the twelfth century the Anglo-Normans removed the *Baculus* to Christ Church Cathedral in Dublin, where it continued to be used to swear witnesses, usually in the presence of the Lord Deputy and Chancellor. Because it was credited with numerous prodigies and miracles, the *Baculus* attracted pilgrims not only from all parts of Ireland but also from other countries, and so became a source of great distinction and emolument for the Cathedral's priory. In 1538 Archbishop Browne, the first Reformation Archbishop of Dublin, caused the *Baculus* to be destroyed publicly in front of the Cathedral.

A less prodigious relic was a bell which, it was believed, had been used by St Patrick; the bronze and silver-gilt shrine made for it *p. 152*
between 1094 and 1105 is now in the National Museum of Ireland.

Among British calendars of the ninth to the eleventh centuries as many as a dozen note the feast of St Patrick on 17 March, while one (from the North of England) has St Patrick on 16 March and St Pancrace on 17 March. Of these calendars, all compiled before 1100, the two earliest, written about 970, are from Glastonbury which claimed to be the place of Patrick's death and attracted many pilgrims from Ireland, and from Westminster. Other calendars are from Wells, Winchester, Sherborne, Ely, Croyland, Bury St Edmunds, and two abbeys tentatively identified as Hyde and Evesham. The name of St Patrick also appears in the late eleventh-century Martyrology from Ricemarsh in Wales. Among the medieval British abbeys claiming to have relics of the Saint were St Albans with his staff, and Waltham in Essex with his dalmatic.

The popularity of devotion to St Patrick in Scotland is attested by the number of place-names there which derive from a dedication to, or an association with the Saint. There are no less than eight: four Kilpatricks, a Kirkpatrick, a Dalpatrick, a Templepatrick and a Portpatrick. This number cannot, of course, vie with the Patrician locative names of Ireland: five parishes and twenty-two townlands named Kilpatrick, two parishes and four townlands named Templepatrick, two townlands and two parishes named Donaghpatrick, three townlands named Toberpatrick and four of the English version of this name, Patrickswell, five townlands named Ballypatrick and one of the English version, Patrickstown, as well as the parish and townland of Holmpatrick which has a direct association with the earliest traditions of the Saint's travels.

Surprisingly, despite the plethora of dedications to Patrick in Ireland, the early genealogies show that Patrick was rarely used as a personal name until the seventeenth century, when it was popularized by the Jacobite hero Patrick Sarsfield. It has since grown so immensely in favour as to become the top favourite. Padraig is the usual form in Irish. The feminine form, Patricia, is a recent innovation in Ireland, no instance of it having been reported there before the last century. Its use as a Christian name appears, in fact, to have begun in Scotland in the eighteenth century, and its present widespread popularity elsewhere to stem from a vogue created by its use in the British royal family for Princess Patricia, a granddaughter of Queen Victoria, born in 1886.

That Patrick was given quite widely as a baptismal name in Scotland and in the North of England by the twelfth century is suggested by the surnames deriving from it that came into use: Patrick, Patrickson, Pate, Patey, Paton and Patton, Pattinson and Pat(t)erson.

In England, Patrick's popularity is attested by the churches that were dedicated to the apostle to the Irish. About a dozen Anglican churches, mostly in the north, are dedicated to St Patrick as well as four in Wales. Roman Catholic churches in Great Britain are mostly of recent date, built over the last one hundred and fifty years to serve communities composed largely of immigrants, most of whom were Irish. It is not surprising, therefore, that about sixty-five of these churches in England and Wales and a further twelve in Scotland are dedicated to the Saint.

Irish monks, indefatigable in their missionary travels through Europe in the early Middle Ages, determined most of the known instances of devotion to St Patrick in France and the lands of Charlemagne's Empire. Frequently they left a relic of their Saint in the custody of the local prelates, better to ensure the continuance of devotion to him in the place. One such early Irish missionary monk was St Fursey, who died in 648 and was buried at Péronne, where his tomb became a centre of pilgrimage. He is said to have brought Patrician relics to Péronne. The Abbot there who died in 706 left an inscription in verse to be used in a chapel dedicated to St Patrick.

The earliest documentary evidence of devotion to St Patrick in France comes from places known to have been frequented by the Irish monks, or along the pilgrimage routes they travelled. Many early manuscript sources in France mention St Patrick (see p. 173), the earliest being the Calendar of St Willibrord, compiled at the beginning of the eighth century at Echternach in Alsace. Patrick is also named in a metric inscription composed by the poet-cleric Alcuin. Alcuin, who was born in England and educated at York, was familiar with Irish-Northumbrian ecclesiastical practice; he lived for many years on the Continent as one of the foremost scholars of his time, and after heading the Palatine school established at Aachen by the Emperor Charlemagne, became the Abbot of the monastery of St Martin at Tours, where he died in 804.

Of the relics of the Saint venerated on the Continent, we know of some brought to Issoudun by refugee monks from Brittany, and of another kept in the Benedictine Abbey of St Pierre at Rheims. At two other places in France, Marmoutier and St Patrice, devotion to St Patrick can be ascribed to a tradition that the Saint himself had visited these spots. We have already learned of the tradition that Patrick sojourned in the monastery founded by St Martin at Marmoutier near Tours; nearby is a rock-hewn cell in the escarpment known as the Grotto of St Patrick, and a bench hewn in the rock is supposed to have served as his bed. At St Patrice, a municipality in the department of Indre-et-Loire, a tradition persists that Patrick was there, and that he used to rest beside a thorn-bush known locally as 'l'épine de Saint Patrice'; it is said that it has flowered every year since at Christmas.

The place known as 'le trou de St Patrice' at La Neuville in the department of Seine-Maritime appears to have once enjoyed the reputation, like St Patrick's Purgatory on Lough Derg, of being an entrance to the underworld; but the reason for the name of St Patrice-en-Mégrit in the Côtes-du-Nord is obscure.

The church dedicated to St Patrick at Rouen has a fine stained-glass window depicting the miracles of the Saint. There is also a chapel dedicated to St Patrick in Brittany at Longuivy-lès-Lannion, and there are at least two private chapels on manorial estates.

References to St Patrick are to be found in the ninth and tenth centuries in manuscripts originating in churches and monasteries east of the Rhine (see p. 173). That the cult of St Patrick was established in Germany at least by the eleventh century is proved by reference to him in several tenth- and eleventh-century liturgical works compiled at Regensburg in Bavaria, where an Irish monk, Marianus Scottus, died as abbot of the Abbey of St Peter in 1088 and also by the dedication of two parish churches: one at Heiligenzimmern in Hohenzollern, consecrated by Eberhard, Bishop of Constance, between 1034 and 1046, and the other at Eitorf in the diocese of Cologne.

At Böhmenkirch in Würtemberg the Chapel of St Patrick has long been a centre of pilgrimages honouring the Saint on his feast day, and at another village church in Würtemberg, at Neubronn near Hohenstadt, a statue of St Patrick is venerated.

In the Austrian province of Styria, St Patrick is honoured as the protector of cattle. At Holleneg in that province, there are three sanctuaries where devotion to St Patrick is practised by pilgrims. At Wenigzell where a Confraternity of St Patrick was established in 1892, St Patrick's chapel in the parish church has a painting depicting the Saint interceding for souls in Purgatory. There is also a St Patrick's chapel with a painting portraying the Saint in the Gothic pilgrimage church at Pollauberg in Styria, built between 1339 and 1374 and later embellished with interior decoration in the Baroque style. Pilgrims at Pollauberg used a work, the *Florilegium Pollense*, prepared in the nearby Abbey of Pollau and printed in 1766, that contains litanies in which Patrick is extolled as a saint who, like Moses, received his staff from the hand of God himself; who saw, in the night, his five fingers change into five suns which illuminated the dark countryside; who delivered souls from Purgatory; and who was the glory and honour of the regular canons of St Augustine.

Beyond the Alps we find evidence of devotion to St Patrick as early as the twelfth century, with the inclusion of his feast day in missals from Cornale and Novacella, near Bressanone in the Italian Tyrol, and in a calendar from Lavant in the same region. Farther south in the peninsula, a church and village dedicated to Patrick, San Patrizio near Conselice in the province of Ravenna, are mentioned in documents of the eleventh and twelfth century. A relic of the Saint is preserved in the chapel dedicated to him at Torre San Patrizio in the province of Ascoli; another relic, described as 'a tooth of St Patrick', is preserved in the Roman church of Santa Maria de Loreto beside the Forum, and another appears on an inventory of relics at Genoa drawn up in 1386. The dedication of a church to St Patrick at Pavia and a well bearing his name at Orvieto are probably due to the presence of Irish pilgrims on their way to Rome.

The principal centre of devotion to St Patrick in Italy outside the Irish foundations in Rome is at Vertova near Bergamo, where the parish church and a sanctuary near the town are dedicated to the Saint. The devotion to St Patrick at Vertova is believed there to be of considerable antiquity, and probably due to the presence at some early date of Irish monks or pilgrims; 17 March was formerly a general holiday in the town, and is still observed as a holiday for the schools. Patrizio is given frequently as a name to children of Vertova families, many of whom have an image of the Saint in their homes. In the sanctuary are frescoes depicting Patrick's miracles, and in the parish church a fine painting by Enea da Salmeggia (1550-1626) depicts St Patrick with the Madonna, St Joseph, St John the Baptist and St Mark.

A general chapter of the Seraphic Order of St Francis convened at Mantova in 1390 decreed that the office of St Patrick should be celebrated by the Order everywhere. This certainly enhanced devotion to the Saint, as did the introduction of his feast to the Roman breviary by Pope Urban VIII in 1631. At that time a universal feast of the Church with a simple rite without lessons because it fell in Lent, it was elevated to the rank of a semi-double rite with nine lessons in 1687 by Pope Innocent XI. It was, however, a book published in Italian at Bologna in 1686 which greatly increased the popularity of St Patrick in Italy. In glorifying and extolling the Saint and in describing the miracles attributed to him, this work, a tome of fourteen chapters by Giacomo Certani, Professor of Moral Philosophy at the University of Bologna, equalled the accounts of imaginative medieval hagiographers; it is entitled *Il Mosé dell' Ibernia, Vita del Glorioso San Patrizio* (The Moses of Hibernia, The Life of the Glorious Saint Patrick), and was translated into German in 1722.

Ceding to the supplications of the Irish hierarchy in 1854 and 1859, the feast of St Patrick was elevated by a decree of Propaganda Fide to its present rank of a double rite, and as such it is universally celebrated in Roman Catholic churches.

The two great spiritual manifestations of the cult of St Patrick today are the pilgrimages to Lough Derg, described in the previous chapter, and the annual pilgrimage to Croaghpatrick, Co. Mayo, 'St Patrick's Reek', where according to the tradition which has come down from the account in the *Tripartite Life*, Patrick, through the intermediary of an Angel, struggled with God to obtain his heart's desire.

plate 17 The Croaghpatrick pilgrimage takes place each year on the last
Sunday in July. The great procession begins before dawn, and the
first Mass of the day, in the oratory erected in 1905 on the summit
of the quartzite cone, is celebrated at five in the morning. Many of
the pilgrims will have begun the steep, arduous ascent on the Saturday night. Tens of thousands of pilgrims make the ascent each year
on that day, the most courageous of them practising mortification by
plate 15 climbing barefoot over the path which is strewn with sharp and
abrasive fragments of quartzite. So rough is the ground that many
pilgrims will carry two pairs of shoes, discarding on their way one
pair rendered useless by the lacerations of the sharp stones. Many of
these discarded shoes, cut and torn, may be seen on the path,
especially on the scree-clad and uppermost reaches before the summit, which is often shrouded in mist. Nevertheless, among the pilgrims each year there are always doughty octagenarians, some of
whom have braved the harsh ordeal as many as forty or fifty times.

Far removed this exercise may seem from the noisy, jolly parades staged in the name of the youth who came to Ireland one thousand five hundred years ago, first as a slave and then as a missionary, but like the secular parades, the pilgrimage is a living witness to the affection which that boy won in the hearts of so many, for so many generations.

The Confessio

1 I, Patrick, a sinner, a most simple countryman, the least of all the faithful and most contemptible to many, had for father the deacon Calpurnius, son of the late Potitus, a priest, of the settlement [*vicus*] of Bannavem Taburniae; he had a small villa nearby where I was taken captive. I was at that time about sixteen years of age. I did not, indeed, know the true God; and I was taken into captivity in Ireland with many thousands of people, according to our deserts, for quite drawn away from God, we did not keep his precepts, nor were we obedient to our priests who used to remind us of our salvation. And the Lord brought down on us the fury of his being and scattered us among many nations, even to the ends of the earth, where I, in my smallness, am now to be found among foreigners.

2 And there the Lord opened my mind to an awareness of my unbelief, in order that, even so late, I might remember my transgressions and turn with all my heart to the Lord my God, who had regard for my insignificance and pitied my youth and ignorance. And he watched over me before I knew him, and before I learned sense or even distinguished between good and evil, and he protected me, and consoled me as a father would his son.

3 Therefore, indeed, I cannot keep silent — nor would it be proper, so many favours and graces has the Lord deigned to bestow on me in the land of my captivity. For after chastisement from God, and recognizing him, our way to repay him is to exalt him and confess his wonders before every nation under heaven.

4 For there is no other God, nor ever was before, nor shall be hereafter, but God the Father, unbegotten and without beginning, in whom all things began, whose are all things, as we have been taught; and his son Jesus Christ, who manifestly always existed with the Father, before the beginning of time in the spirit with the Father, indescribably begotten before all things, and all things visible and invisible were made by him. He was made man, conquered death and was received into Heaven, to the Father who gave him all power over every name in Heaven and on Earth and in Hell, so that every tongue should confess that Jesus Christ is Lord and God, in whom we believe. And we look to his imminent coming again, the judge of the living and the dead, who will render to each according to his deeds. And he poured out his Holy Spirit on us in abundance, the gift and pledge of immortality, which makes the believers and the obedient into sons of God and co-heirs of

Christ who is revealed, and we worship one God in the Trinity of holy name.

5 He himself said through the prophet: 'Call upon me in the day of trouble; I will deliver you, and you shall glorify me.' [1] And again: 'It is right to reveal and publish abroad the works of God.' [2]

6 I am imperfect in many things, nevertheless I want my brethren and kinsfolk to know my nature so that they may be able to perceive my soul's desire.

7 I am not ignorant of what is said of my Lord in the Psalm: 'You destroy those who speak a lie.' [3] And again: 'A lying mouth deals death to the soul.' [4] And likewise the Lord says in the Gospel: 'On the day of judgment men shall render account for every idle word they utter.' [5]

8 So it is that I should mightily fear, with terror and trembling, this judgment on the day when no one shall be able to steal away or hide, but each and all shall render account for even our smallest sins before the judgment seat of Christ the Lord.

9 And therefore for some time I have thought of writing, but I have hesitated until now, for truly, I feared to expose myself to the criticism of men, because I have not studied like others, who have assimilated both Law and the Holy Scriptures equally and have never changed their idiom since their infancy, but instead were always learning it increasingly, to perfection, while my idiom and language have been translated into a foreign tongue. So it is easy to prove from a sample of my writing, my ability in rhetoric and the extent of my preparation and knowledge, for as it is said, 'wisdom shall be recognized in speech, and in understanding, and in knowledge and in the learning of truth.' [6]

10 But why make excuses close to the truth, especially when now I am presuming to try to grasp in my old age what I did not gain in my youth because my sins prevented me from making what I had read my own? But who will believe me, even though I should say it again? A young man, almost a beardless boy, I was taken captive before I knew what I should desire and what I should shun. So, consequently, today I feel ashamed and I am mightily afraid to expose my ignorance, because, [not] eloquent, with a small vocabulary, I am unable to explain as the spirit is eager to do and as the soul and the mind indicate.

11 But had it been given to me as to others, in gratitude I should not have kept silent, and if it should appear that I put myself before others, with my ignorance and my slower speech, in truth, it is written: 'The tongue of the stammerers shall speak rapidly and distinctly.' [7] How much harder must we try to attain it, we of whom it is said: 'You are an epistle of Christ in greeting to the ends of the earth … written on your hearts, not with ink but with the Spirit of the living God.' [8] And again, the Spirit witnessed that the rustic life was created by the Most High. [9]

1 Psalms 50:15   2 Tobit 12:7   3 Psalms 5:6   4 Wisdom 1:11
5 Matthew 12:36   6 Partly Ecclesiasticus 4:29   7 Isaiah 32:4
8 II Corinthians 3:3   9 Ecclesiasticus 7:6

12 I am, then, first of all, countryfied, an exile, evidently unlearned, one who is not able to see into the future, but I know for certain, that before I was humbled I was like a stone lying in deep mire, and he that is mighty came and in his mercy raised me up and, indeed, lifted me high up and placed me on top of the wall. And from there I ought to shout out in gratitude to the Lord for his great favours in this world and for ever, that the mind of man cannot measure.

13 Therefore be amazed, you great and small who fear God, and you men of God, eloquent speakers, listen and contemplate. Who was it summoned me, a fool, from the midst of those who appear wise and learned in the law and powerful in rhetoric and in all things? Me, truly wretched in this world, he inspired before others that I could be – if I would – such a one who, with fear and reverence, and faithfully, without complaint, would come to the people to whom the love of Christ brought me and gave me in my lifetime, if I should be worthy, to serve them truly and with humility.

14 According, therefore, to the measure of one's faith in the Trinity, one should proceed without holding back from danger to make known the gift of God and everlasting consolation, to spread God's name everywhere with confidence and without fear, in order to leave behind, after my death, foundations for my brethren and sons whom I baptized in the Lord in so many thousands.

15 And I was not worthy, nor was I such that the Lord should grant his humble servant this, that after hardships and such great trials, after captivity, after many years, he should give me so much favour in these people, a thing which in the time of my youth I neither hoped for nor imagined.

16 But after I reached Ireland I used to pasture the flock each day and I used to pray many times a day. More and more did the love of God, and my fear of him and faith increase, and my spirit was moved so that in a day [I said] from one up to a hundred prayers, and in the night a like number; besides I used to stay out in the forests and on the mountain and I would wake up before daylight to pray in the snow, in icy coldness, in rain, and I used to feel neither ill nor any slothfulness, because, as I now see, the Spirit was burning in me at that time.

17 And it was there of course that one night in my sleep I heard a voice saying to me: 'You do well to fast: soon you will depart for your home country.' And again, a very short time later, there was a voice prophesying: 'Behold, your ship is ready.' And it was not close by, but, as it happened, two hundred miles away, where I had never been nor knew any person. And shortly thereafter I turned about and fled from the man with whom I had been for six years, and I came, by the power of God who directed my route to advantage (and I was afraid of nothing), until I reached that ship.

18 And on the same day that I arrived, the ship was setting out from the place, and I said that I had the wherewithal to sail with them; and the steersman was displeased and replied in anger, sharply: 'By no means attempt to go with us.' Hearing this I left them to go to the hut where I was staying, and on the way I began to pray, and before the prayer was finished I

heard one of them shouting loudly after me: 'Come quickly because the men are calling you.' And immediately I went back to them and they started to say to me: 'Come, because we are admitting you out of good faith; make friendship with us in any way you wish.' (And so, on that day, I refused to suck the breasts of these men from fear of God, but nevertheless I had hopes that they would come to faith in Jesus Christ, because they were barbarians.) And for this I continued with them, and forthwith we put to sea.
19 And after three days we reached land, and for twenty-eight days journeyed through uninhabited country, and the food ran out and hunger overtook them; and one day the steersman began saying: 'Why is it, Christian? You say your God is great and all-powerful; then why can you not pray for us? For we may perish of hunger; it is unlikely indeed that we shall ever see another human being.' In fact, I said to them, confidently: 'Be converted by faith with all your heart to my Lord God, because nothing is impossible for him, so that today he will send food for you on your road, until you be sated, because everywhere he abounds.' And with God's help this came to pass; and behold, a herd of swine appeared on the road before our eyes, and they slew many of them, and remained there for two nights, and they were full of their meat and well restored, for many of them had fainted and would otherwise have been left half dead by the wayside. And after this they gave the utmost thanks to God, and I was esteemed in their eyes, and from that day they had food abundantly. They discovered wild honey, besides, and they offered a share to me, and one of them said: 'It is a sacrifice.' Thanks be to God, I tasted none of it.
20 The very same night while I was sleeping Satan attacked me violently, as I will remember as long as I shall be in this body; and there fell on top of me as it were, a huge rock, and not one of my members had any force. But from whence did it come to me, ignorant in the spirit, to call upon 'Helias'? And meanwhile I saw the sun rising in the sky, and while I was crying out 'Helias, Helias' with all my might, lo, the brilliance of that sun fell upon me and immediately shook me free of all the weight; and I believe that I was aided by Christ my Lord, and that his Spirit then was crying out for me, and I hope that it will be so in the day of my affliction, just as it says in the Gospel: 'In that hour', the Lord declares, 'it is not you who speaks but the Spirit of your Father speaking in you.'[10]
21 (And a second time, after many years, I was taken captive. On the first night I accordingly remained with my captors, but I heard a divine prophecy, saying to me: 'You shall be with them for two months. So it happened. On the sixtieth night the Lord delivered me from their hands.)
22 On the journey he provided us with food and fire and dry weather every day, until on the tenth day we came upon people. As I mentioned above, we had journeyed through an unpopulated country for twenty-eight days, and in fact the night that we came upon people we had no food.

10 Matthew 10:19–20

23 And after a few years I was again in Britain with my parents [kinsfolk], and they welcomed me as a son, and asked me, in faith, that after the great tribulations I had endured I should not go anywhere else away from them. And, of course, there, in a vision of the night, I saw a man whose name was Victoricus coming as if from Ireland with innumerable letters, and he gave me one of them, and I read the beginning of the letter: 'The Voice of the Irish', and as I was reading the beginning of the letter I seemed at that moment to hear the voice of those who were beside the forest of Foclut which is near the western sea, and they were crying as if with one voice: 'We beg you, holy youth, that you shall come and shall walk again among us.' And I was stung intensely in my heart so that I could read no more, and thus I awoke. Thanks be to God, because after so many years the Lord bestowed on them according to their cry.

24 And another night – God knows, I do not, whether within me or beside me – ... most words + ... + which I heard and could not understand, except at the end of the speech it was represented thus: 'He who gave his life for you, he it is who speaks within you.' And thus I awoke, joyful.

25 And on a second occasion I saw Him praying within me, and I was as it were, inside my own body, and I heard Him above me – that is, above my inner self. He was praying powerfully with sighs. And in the course of this I was astonished and wondering, and I pondered who it could be who was praying within me. But at the end of the prayer it was revealed to me that it was the Spirit. And so I awoke and remembered the Apostle's words: 'Likewise the Spirit helps us in our weakness; for we know not how to pray as we ought. But the Spirit Himself intercedes for us with sighs too deep for utterance.'[11] And again: 'The Lord our advocate intercedes for us.'[12]

26 And then I was attacked by a goodly number of my elders, who [brought up] my sins against my arduous episcopate. That day in particular I was mightily upset, and might have fallen here and for ever; but the Lord generously spared me, a convert, and an alien, for his name's sake, and he came powerfully to my assistance in that state of being trampled down. I pray God that it shall not be held against them as a sin that I fell truly into disgrace and scandal.

27 They brought up against me after thirty years an occurrence I had confessed before becoming a deacon. On account of the anxiety in my sorrowful mind, I laid before my close friend what I had perpetrated on a day – nay, rather in one hour – in my boyhood because I was not yet proof against sin. God knows – I do not – whether I was fifteen years old at the time, and I did not then believe in the living God, nor had I believed, since my infancy; but I remained in death and unbelief until I was severely rebuked, and in truth I was humbled every day by hunger and nakedness.

28 On the other hand, I did not proceed to Ireland of my own accord until I was almost giving up, but through this I was corrected by the Lord, and he prepared me so that today I should be what was once far from me, in order

11 Romans 8:26 12 *cf.* I John 2:1

that I should have the care of — or rather, I should be concerned for — the salvation of others, when at that time, still, I was only concerned for myself.

29 Therefore, on that day when I was rebuked, as I have just mentioned, I saw in a vision of the night a document before my face, without honour, and meanwhile I heard a divine prophecy, saying to me: 'We have seen with displeasure the face of the chosen one divested of [his good] name.' And he did not say 'You have seen with displeasure', but 'We have seen with displeasure' (as if He included Himself). He said then: 'He who touches you, touches the apple of my eye.'[13]

30 For that reason, I give thanks to him who strengthened me in all things, so that I should not be hindered in my setting out and also in my work which I was taught by Christ my Lord; but more, from that state of affairs I felt, within me, no little courage, and vindicated my faith before God and man.

31 Hence, therefore, I say boldly that my conscience is clear now and hereafter. God is my witness that I have not lied in these words to you.

32 But rather, I am grieved for my very close friend, that because of him we deserved to hear such a prophecy. The one to whom I entrusted my soul! And I found out from a goodly number of brethren, before the case was made in my defence (in which I did not take part, nor was I in Britain, nor was it pleaded by me), that in my absence he would fight in my behalf. Besides, he told me himself: 'See, the rank of bishop goes to you' – of which I was not worthy. But how did it come to him, shortly afterwards, to disgrace me publicly, in the presence of all, good and bad, because previously, gladly and of his own free will, he pardoned me, as did the Lord, who is greater than all?

33 I have said enough. But all the same, I ought not to conceal God's gift which he lavished on us in the land of my captivity, for then I sought him resolutely, and I found him there, and he preserved me from all evils (as I believe) through the in-dwelling of his Spirit, which works in me to this day. Again, boldly, but God knows, if this had been made known to me by man, I might, perhaps, have kept silent for the love of Christ.

34 Thus I give untiring thanks to God who kept me faithful in the day of my temptation, so that today I may confidently offer my soul as a living sacrifice for Christ my Lord; who am I, Lord? or, rather, what is my calling? that you appeared to me in so great a divine quality, so that today among the barbarians I might constantly exalt and magnify your name in whatever place I should be, and not only in good fortune, but even in affliction? So that whatever befalls me, be it good or bad, I should accept it equally, and give thanks always to God who revealed to me that I might trust in him, implicitly and forever, and who will encourage me so that, ignorant, and in the last days, I may dare to undertake so devout and so wonderful a work; so that I might imitate one of those whom, once, long ago, the Lord already pre-ordained to be heralds of his Gospel to witness to all peoples to the ends of the earth. So are we seeing, and so it is fulfilled; behold, we are witnesses

13 Zechariah 2:8

because the Gospel has been preached as far as the places beyond which no man lives.

35 But it is tedious to describe in detail all my labours one by one. I will tell briefly how most holy God frequently delivered me, from slavery, and from the twelve trials with which my soul was threatened, from many traps as well, and from things I am not able to put into words. I would not cause offence to readers, but I have God as witness who knew all things even before they happened, that, though I was a poor ignorant waif, still he gave me abundant warnings through divine prophecy.

36 Whence came to me this wisdom which was not my own, I who neither knew the number of days nor had knowledge of God? Whence came the so great and so healthful gift of knowing or rather loving God, though I should lose homeland and family.

37 And many gifts were offered to me with weeping and tears, and I offended them [the donors], and also went against the wishes of a good number of my elders; but guided by God, I neither agreed with them nor deferred to them, not by my own grace but by God who is victorious in me and withstands them all, so that I might come to the Irish people to preach the Gospel and endure insults from unbelievers; that I might hear scandal of my travels, and endure many persecutions to the extent of prison; and so that I might give up my free birthright for the advantage of others, and if I should be worthy, I am ready [to give] even my life without hesitation and most willingly for His name. And I choose to devote it to him even unto death, if God grant it to me.

38 I am greatly God's debtor, because he granted me so much grace, that through me many people would be reborn in God, and soon after confirmed, and that clergy would be ordained everywhere for them, the masses lately come to belief, whom the Lord drew from the ends of the earth, just as he once promised through his prophets: 'To you shall the nations come from the ends of the earth, and shall say, Our fathers have inherited naught but lies, worthless things in which there is no profit.'[14] And again: 'I have set you to be a light for the Gentiles that you may bring salvation to the uttermost ends of the earth.'[15]

39 And I wish to wait then for his promise which is never unfulfilled, just as it is promised in the Gospel: 'Many shall come from east and west and shall sit at table with Abraham and Isaac and Jacob.'[16] Just as we believe that believers will come from all the world.

40 So for that reason one should, in fact, fish well and diligently, just as the Lord foretells and teaches, saying, 'Follow me, and I will make you fishers of men,'[17] and again through the prophets: 'Behold, I am sending forth many fishers and hunters, says the Lord,'[18] et cetera. So it behoved us to spread our nets, that a vast multitude and throng might be caught for God, and so

14 Jeremiah 16:19 15 Acts 13:47 16 Matthew 8:11
17 Matthew 4:19 18 Jeremiah 16:16

there might be clergy everywhere who baptized and exhorted a needy and desirous people. Just as the Lord says in the Gospel, admonishing and instructing: 'Go therefore and make disciples of all nations, baptizing them in the name of the Father and of the Son and of the Holy Spirit, teaching them to observe all that I have commanded you; and lo, I am with you always to the end of time.'[19] And again he says: 'Go forth into the world and preach the Gospel to all creation. He who believes and is baptized shall be saved; but he who does not believe shall be condemned.'[20] And again: 'This Gospel of the Kingdom shall be preached throughout the whole world as a witness to all nations; and then the end of the world shall come.'[21] And likewise the Lord foretells through the prophet: 'And it shall come to pass in the last days (sayeth the Lord) that I will pour out my spirit upon all flesh, and your sons and daughters shall prophesy, and your young men shall see visions and your old men shall dream dreams; yea, and on my menservants and my maidservants in those days I will pour out my Spirit and they shall prophesy.'[22] And in Hosea he says: 'Those who are not my people I will call my people, and those not beloved I will call my beloved, and in the very place where it was said to them, You are not my people, they will be called 'Sons of the living God'.[23]

41 So, how is it that in Ireland, where they never had any knowledge of God but, always, until now, cherished idols and unclean things, they are lately become a people of the Lord, and are called children of God; the sons of the Irish [Scotti] and the daughters of the chieftains are to be seen as monks and virgins of Christ.

42 And there was, besides, a most beautiful, blessed, native-born noble Irish [Scotta] woman of adult age whom I baptized; and a few days later she had reason to come to us to intimate that she had received a prophecy from a divine messenger [who] advised her that she should become a virgin of Christ and she would draw nearer to God. Thanks be to God, six days from then, opportunely and most eagerly, she took the course that all virgins of God take, not with their fathers' consent but enduring the persecutions and deceitful hindrances of their parents. Notwithstanding that, their number increases, (we do not know the number of them that are so reborn) besides the widows, and those who practise self-denial. Those who are kept in slavery suffer the most. They endure terrors and constant threats, but the Lord has given grace to many of his handmaidens, for even though they are forbidden to do so, still they resolutely follow his example.

43 So it is that even if I should wish to separate from them in order to go to Britain, and most willingly was I prepared to go to my homeland and kinsfolk – and not only there, but as far as Gaul to visit the brethren there, so that I might see the faces of the holy ones of my Lord, God knows how strongly I desired this – I am bound by the Spirit, who witnessed to me that

19 Matthew 28:19, 20 Mark 16:15, 16 21 Matthew 24:14
22 Acts 2:17–18; Joel 2:28, 9 23 Romans 9:25–6; *cf.* Hosea 1:9–10

if I did so he would mark me out as guilty, and I fear to waste the labour that I began, and not I, but Christ the Lord, who commanded me to come to be with them for the rest of my life, if the Lord shall will it and shield me from every evil, so that I may not sin before him.

44 So I hope that I did as I ought, but I do not trust myself as long as I am in this mortal body, for he is strong who strives daily to turn me away from the faith and true holiness to which I aspire until the end of my life for Christ my Lord, but the hostile flesh is always dragging one down to death, that is, to unlawful attractions. And I know in part why I did not lead a perfect life like other believers, but I confess to my Lord and do not blush in his sight, because I am not lying; from the time when I came to know him in my youth, the love of God and fear of him increased in me, and right up until now, by God's favour, I have kept the faith.

45 What is more, let anyone laugh and taunt if he so wishes. I am not keeping silent, nor am I hiding the signs and wonders that were shown to me by the Lord many years before they happened, [he] who knew everything, even before the beginning of time.

46 Thus, I should give thanks unceasingly to God, who frequently forgave my folly and my negligence, in more than one instance so as not to be violently angry with me, who am placed as his helper, and I did not easily assent to what had been revealed to me, as the Spirit was urging; and the Lord took pity on me thousands upon thousands of times, because he saw within me that I was prepared, but that I was ignorant of what to do in view of my situation; because many were trying to prevent this mission. They were talking among themselves behind my back, and saying: 'Why is this fellow throwing himself into danger among enemies who know not God?' Not from malice, but having no liking for it; likewise, as I myself can testify, they perceived my rusticity. And I was not quick to recognize the grace that was then in me; I now know that I should have done so earlier.

47 Now I have put it frankly to my brethren and co-workers, who have believed me because of what I have foretold and still foretell to strengthen and reinforce your faith. I wish only that you, too, would make greater and better efforts. This will be my pride, for 'a wise son makes a proud father'.[24]

48 You know, as God does, how I went about among you from my youth in the faith of truth and in sincerity of heart. As well as to the heathen among whom I live, I have shown them trust and always show them trust. God knows I did not cheat any one of them, nor consider it, for the sake of God and his Church, lest I arouse them and [bring about] persecution for them and for all of us, and lest the Lord's name be blasphemed because of me, for it is written: 'Woe to the men through whom the name of the Lord is blasphemed.'[25]

49 For even though I am ignorant in all things, nevertheless I attempted to safeguard some and myself also. And I gave back again to my Christian brethren and the virgins of Christ and the holy women the small unasked for

24 Proverbs 10:1 25 *cf.* Matthew 18:7

gifts that they used to give me or some of their ornaments which they used to throw on the altar. And they would be offended with me because I did this. But in the hope of eternity, I safeguarded myself carefully in all things, so that they might not cheat me of my office of service on any pretext of dishonesty, and so that I should not in the smallest way provide any occasion for defamation or disparagement on the part of unbelievers.

50 What is more, when I baptized so many thousands of people, did I hope for even half a jot from any of them? [If so] Tell me, and I will give it back to you. And when the Lord ordained clergy everywhere by my humble means, and I freely conferred office on them, if I asked any of them anywhere even for the price of one shoe, say so to my face and I will give it back.

51 More, I spent for you so that they would receive me. And I went about among you, and everywhere for your sake, in danger, and as far as the outermost regions beyond which no one lived, and where no one had ever penetrated before, to baptize or to ordain clergy or to confirm people. Conscientiously and gladly I did all this work by God's gift for your salvation.

52 From time to time I gave rewards to the kings, as well as making payments to their sons who travel with me; notwithstanding which, they seized me with my companions, and that day most avidly desired to kill me. But my time had not yet come. They plundered everything they found on us anyway, and fettered me in irons; and on the fourteenth day the Lord freed me from their power, and whatever they had of ours was given back to us for the sake of God on account of the indispensable friends whom we had made before.

53 Also you know from experience how much I was paying to those who were administering justice in all the regions, which I visited often. I estimate truly that I distributed to them not less than the price of fifteen men, in order that you should enjoy my company and I enjoy yours, always, in God. I do not regret this nor do I regard it as enough. I am paying out still and I shall pay out more. The Lord has the power to grant me that I may soon spend my own self, for your souls.

54 Behold, I call on God as my witness upon my soul that I am not lying; nor would I write to you for it to be an occasion for flattery or selfishness, nor hoping for honour from any one of you. Sufficient is the honour which is not yet seen, but in which the heart has confidence. He who made the promise is faithful; he never lies.

55 But I see that even here and now, I have been exalted beyond measure by the Lord, and I was not worthy that he should grant me this, while I know most certainly that poverty and failure suit me better than wealth and delight (but Christ the Lord was poor for our sakes; I certainly am wretched and unfortunate; even if I wanted wealth I have no resources), nor is it my own estimation of myself, for daily I expect to be murdered or betrayed or reduced to slavery if the occasion arises. But I fear nothing, because of the promises of Heaven; for I have cast myself into the hands of Almighty God, who reigns everywhere. As the prophet says: 'Cast your burden on the Lord and he will sustain you.'[26]

56 Behold now I commend my soul to God who is most faithful and for whom I perform my mission in obscurity, but he is no respecter of persons and he chose me for this service that I might be one of the least of his ministers.

57 For which reason I should make return for all that he returns me. But what should I say, or what should I promise to my Lord, for I, alone, can do nothing unless he himself vouchsafe it to me. But let him search my heart and [my] nature, for I crave enough for it, even too much, and I am ready for him to grant me that I drink of his chalice, as he has granted to others who love him.

58 Therefore may it never befall me to be separated by my God from his people whom he has won in this most remote land. I pray God that he gives me perseverance, and that he will deign that I should be a faithful witness for his sake right up to the time of my passing.

59 And if at any time I managed anything of good for the sake of my God whom I love, I beg of him that he grant it to me to shed my blood for his name with proselytes and captives, even should I be left unburied, or even were my wretched body to be torn limb from limb by dogs or savage beasts, or were it to be devoured by the birds of the air, I think, most surely, were this to have happened to me, I had saved both my soul and my body. For beyond any doubt on that day we shall rise again in the brightness of the sun, that is, in the glory of Christ Jesus our Redeemer, as children of the living God and co-heirs of Christ, made in his image; for we shall reign through him and for him and in him.

60 For the sun we see rises each day for us at [his] command, but it will never reign, neither will its splendour last, but all who worship it will come wretchedly to punishment. We, on the other hand, shall not die, who believe in and worship the true sun, Christ, who will never die, no more shall he die who has done Christ's will, but will abide for ever just as Christ abides for ever, who reigns with God the Father Almighty and with the Holy Spirit before the beginning of time and now and for ever and ever. Amen.

61 Behold over and over again I would briefly set out the words of my confession. I testify in truthfulness and gladness of heart before God and his holy angels that I never had any reason, except the Gospel and his promises, ever to have returned to that nation from which I had previously escaped with difficulty.

62 But I entreat those who believe in and fear God, whoever deigns to examine or receive this document composed by the obviously unlearned sinner Patrick in Ireland, that nobody shall ever ascribe to my ignorance any trivial thing that I achieved or may have expounded that was pleasing to God, but accept and truly believe that it would have been the gift of God. And this is my confession before I die.

26 Psalms 55:2

The Letter to Coroticus

1 I, Patrick, a sinner, established in Ireland, manifestly unlearned, am acknowledged to be a bishop. Most certainly, I have accepted that which I am by God's merit. And thus I live among barbarian peoples, a stranger and an exile for the love of God. He is my witness that this is so. I did not wish to give vent to something so harsh and so severe from my lips, but I am forced to do so by my zeal for God, and Christ's truth has inspired me, for love of my neighbours and also of my children, for whom I gave up homeland and family [and gave of] myself even to death. If I am worthy I live for God, to teach the people, even if some despise me.

2 I have composed these words and written them with my own hand, to be sent, delivered and put into the hands of the soldiers of Coroticus — I do not say to [be sent to] my fellow-citizens nor to the citizens of the venerable Romans, but to the citizens of the demons, because of their evil doings. They live in the way the enemy does, in death, companions of the Irish [Scotti], and of the Picts, and of apostates; bloodthirsty to sate themselves with the innocent blood of countless Christians whom I begot for God and confirmed in Christ besides.

3 On the very day after the neophytes had been chrismed in their white robes and [while] the holy chrism was still glowing on their foreheads, they were slaughtered and sacrificed too by the swords of those aforementioned. I sent a letter with a holy priest whom I had taught since his childhood, with some clerics, [requesting that] they should grant us some of the spoils they had taken and the baptized persons whom they had taken into bondage; they laughed immoderately at us.

4 On that account, I know not whom they deplore the more, whether it is those who have been massacred, or those who have been abducted by force, or those whom the evil one has vehemently ensnared. They themselves shall be delivered up to everlasting punishment likewise, because whoever sins is a servant of the evil one, and shall be proclaimed to be his son.

5 Wherefore, let all who fear God know that they are estranged from me and from Christ my God, whose deputed representative I am: the murderer of father, of brother, rapacious wolves devouring the people of God like so much bread; as it is said, 'The wicked have broken thy law, O Lord;[1] which

1 *cf.* Psalm 118:126

in these last days he had liberally planted in Ireland and established according to God's favour.

6 I am not laying a claim unjustly; I have a share with those whom he called and predestined to preach the Gospel amid no little persecution to the ends of the earth, even though the enemy, by the tyrant Coroticus, casts his evil eye, not fearing God nor his priests whom he has chosen, and to whom he has granted the highest, divine, sublime power, that those whom they bind on earth shall be bound in Heaven.

7 Wherefore, I ardently plead with the virtuous and humble of heart: it is not lawful to flatter such as these, nor to partake of food or drink with them, nor should alms be accepted from them, until such time as they satisfy God by the most abject penance and shedding of tears, and liberate the servants of God and the baptized handmaidens of Christ for whom he died and was crucified.

8 'The Most High is not pleased with the offerings of the ungodly.'[2] 'Like one who kills a son before his father's eyes is the man who offers a sacrifice from the property of the poor.'[3] It is said, 'He swallows down unjustly amassed riches and vomits them up again; God casts them out of his belly'[4] — 'The angel of death will drag him away' — 'He will be subjected to the fury of dragons' — 'The tongue of a viper will kill him'[5] — 'An unquenchable fire will devour him.'[6] And likewise: 'Woe to him who heaps up what is not his own'[7]— or, if you wish: 'For what will it profit a man, if he gains the whole world and forfeits his own soul.'[8]

9 It is tedious to discuss or bring up each individual point, to gather evidence of such cupidity from the whole law. Avarice is a mortal sin. 'You shall not covet your neighbour's goods.'[9] 'You shall not kill.'[10] A murderer cannot be with Christ. 'He who hates his brother is a murderer'[11] — and: 'He who does not love his brother remains in death.'[12] How much more guilty is he who has defiled his hands with the blood of the sons of God, not long won over to him at the ends of the earth through our humble exhortation.

10 Did I come to Ireland without God, or according to the flesh? Who compelled me? I am bound by the Spirit not to see any of my own kindred. Is it at all from myself that I can show kindness and mercy to the very people who once abducted me and ravaged the slaves and handmaidens of my father's house? By the flesh I was free-born; I was born of a father who was a decurion. I sold my noble rank, to be sure — not that I blush for that, nor do I regret it — [it was] for the advantage of others. In the end, I am a slave in Christ to a foreign people for the ineffable glory of life everlasting which is in Christ Jesus our Lord.

11 And if my own do not recognize me, a prophet does not have honour in his own country. In truth, we are not all sheep of one fold, nor have we all

2 Sirach 34:19 3 Sirach 34:20 4 Job 20:15 5 Job 20:16 6 Job 20:26
7 Habakkuk 2:6 8 Matthew 16:26 9 Exodus 20:17 10 Exodus 20:13
11 1 John 3:15 12 1 John 3:14

one God for father, just as it is said, 'He who is not with me is against me, and he who does not gather with me scatters.'[13]. We are not in harmony: one destroys, the other constructs. I am nat begging for what is my own. It is not my grace, but God who put this anxiety in my heart to be one of his hunters or fishers, of whom God foretold in the last days.

12 I am envied. What should I do O Lord? I am greatly despised. Behold your sheep are torn to pieces around me, they are carried off, and by the aforementioned brigands, in obedience to the hostile design of Coroticus. Far from God's love is he who delivers Christians into the hands of the Irish [Scottorum] and of the Picts. Ravening wolves have devoured the Lord's flock that, especially in Ireland, was growing with the utmost diligence. And I cannot count the number of monks and virgins of Christ [among] the sons of the Irish [Scottorum] and the daughters of the Kings. Indeed, let not the injustice to the righteous be pleasing to you: even as far as hell it shall not be pleasing.

13 Which of the saints would not shudder [at the thought] of merriment with such as these or feasting with them. They have replenished their homes with the spoils from dead Christians. They live by plunder. The wretches do not know that they are proffering to their friends and to their children food that is deadly poison, just as Eve did not perceive the she was handing death to her husband. So it is for all those who do evil; they will reap the punishment of eternal death.

14 According to their custom the Roman Christians of Gaul send suitable holy men to the Franks and other peoples with many thousands of coins [*solidorum*] to buy back the baptized captives. You prefer to kill them, and sell them to foreign peoples who do not know God; you deliver up the members of Christ, so to speak to a brothel. What hope have you in God, or has he who agrees with you, or speaks flattering words to you? God will judge. Yes, indeed, it is written: 'Not only those who do evil deserve to die, but also those who approved will be damned.'[14]

15 I know not what more I can say or tell of the deceased sons of God whom the sword struck too hard. Yes, indeed, it is written: 'Weep with those who weep;[15] and again: 'If one member suffers, all suffer together.'[16] On that account the Church weeps for and bewails her sons and daughers, who are not yet put to the sword but are taken far away, and carried off to distant lands where sin plainly abounds shamelessly and mightily; where free-born men have been sold, Christians are brought to slavery, especially [as slaves] of the most unworthy, most evil and apostate Picts.

16 For this reason I shall cry out aloud in sadness and grief. O most beautiful and indeed most beloved brothers and children whom I begot in Christ (I cannot count your number), what can I do for you? I am not worthy to come to the aid of God or man. The iniquity of the iniquitous has prevailed over us. We have become as strangers. Perhaps they do not believe

13 Matthew 12:30 14 *cf.* Romans 1:32 15 Romans 12:15
16 1 Corinthians 12:26

that we are brought together in one baptism or that we have one God for Father. It is of no worth to them that we are Irish ['Hiberionaci' or 'Hiberia nati']. Just as it is written: 'Have you not all one God? Why then have you one and all abandoned your neighbour?'[17]

17 For this reason I am suffering for you, I am suffering, my dearest ones. But, again, I rejoice within myself: I did not labour for nothing, nor has my living abroad been in vain. And such a horrendous, unutterable, evil deed took place; thanks be to God you left this world for paradise as baptized believers. I can see you distinctly, you have begun your journey to where there will be no night nor sorrowing nor death any more, but you will exult like calves freed of their bonds and you will trample down the wicked and they will be ashes under your feet.

18 Wherefore, you will reign with the apostles and prophets and with the martyrs also. You will reach the Eternal Kingdom, just as he himself vouched. It is written: 'Many will come from east and west and sit down at table with Abraham, Isaac and Jacob in the kingdom of heaven.'[18] 'Outside are the dogs and sorcerers and murderers',[19] and 'But as for the liars and perjurors their lot shall be in the lake that burns with everlasting fire.'[20] Not without cause the apostle said: 'And if the righteous man is scarcely saved, where will the sinner and the impious law-breaker find himself?'

19 What, then, of Coroticus indeed, with his most infamous criminals, rebels against Christ, where are they to see themselves, they who portion out baptized women as prizes, for the sake of a wretched earthly kingdom that shall soon pass away? Like clouds of smoke scattered by the wind, deceitful sinners shall perish before the force of the Lord. While the righteous, in full steadfastness, shall be present at the banqueting table with Christ; they shall judge nations and shall have dominion over wicked Kings for ever and ever. Amen.

20 I bear witness before God and his angels that it will be thus, just as he made it known to me in my ignorance. It is not my word that I set forth in Latin, but [the word] of God, and of the apostles, and of the prophets, who, indeed, have certainly not lied. 'He who believes will be saved, but he who does not believe will be condemned.'[21] God has spoken.

21 I beg most ardently that whichever servant of God shall be ready, he shall be the bearer of this letter in order that it shall by no means pass unnoticed or be concealed by any man, but shall rather be read out before the entire people, and in the presence of Coroticus himself. That if God inspires them, and at whatsoever time they come back to their senses in God, that thus even late they might repent, and free the baptized captive women whom they have seized, so that they might be worthy to live in God and be made whole now and forever. Peace to the Father, to the Son and to the Holy Spirit.

17 Matthew 8:11 18 Revelation 22:15 19 *cf.* Revelation 21:8
20 1 Peter 4:18 21 Mark 16:16

Notes on Illustrations

Numbers at left refer to pages

2 St Patrick's Well, a beauty-spot two miles west of Clonmel, Co. Tipperary, adjacent to the demesne of Oaklands — an abundant spring long traditionally associated with St Patrick. Beside the well stands a ruined medieval church. A statue of the Saint was erected in 1956, and the site was repaired by the St Patrick's Day Society in 1967–9 with financial help from the Irish-Israeli Society of Southern California and the Mayor of Los Angeles.

6 Detail of a mosaic floor with the head of Christ, the earliest known British depiction, from a villa at Hinton St Mary, 4th century. British Museum.

12 Orantes, Christian worshippers making a gesture of prayer. Drawing after the wall-painting in the chapel of the Roman villa at Lullingstone, Kent, 4th century. British Museum.

20 Mithras slaying the bull, marble relief from a temple of Mithras, Wallbrook, London, late 2nd or 3rd century AD. The Museum of London.

22 A slave-boy in Roman Britain. Bronze oil-lamp from Aldborough, Yorkshire, 2nd century AD. British Museum.

24 The Hill of Tara, Co. Meath, from an aerial view of the earthworks of the hill-fort. Director in Aerial photography, University of Cambridge.

34 The 'Angel's footprint' on the hillside of Skerry, Co. Antrim, from a photograph by George Mott.

38 Shrine of St Patrick's bell, made for a bell reputed to have been the Saint's own at Armagh, bronze and silver gilt, 10th-11th century. National Museum of Ireland.

42 Church of Ireland church, Saul, Co. Down, from a photograph by George Mott.

43 Commemorative statue of St Patrick on Slieve Patrick, Co. Down, from a photograph by George Mott.

44 Struel Wells, the old chapel and the two wells, engraving from *The Holy Wells of Ireland*, Philip Dixon Hardy, 1836.

52 Forest on the Hill of Uisneach, from a photograph by George Mott.

70 Pagan idol of the Celtic era, in the cemetery of Boa Island, Lough Erne, Co. Fermanagh.

78 'St Patrick', 'Enna' and 'Loegaire'. Early Christian stone figures on the wall of the ruined church at White Island, Lough Erne, Co. Fermanagh.

106 Stone over the supposed tomb of Patrick, Downpatrick, Co. Down, from a photograph by George Mott.

110 Devotional stone asking the blessing of St Patrick Station Island, Lough Derg, from a photograph by George Mott. See p. 127 below.

114 The Prior of St Patrick's Purgatory giving instruction to Knight Owen. Woodcut from a book on the Purgatory printed in Lyons in 1506. Bibliothèque Nationale, Paris.

117 St Patrick revealing Purgatory. Miniature from a medieval version of Henry of Saltrey's *Tract*, in Fonds

Français, MS 13496, Bibliothèque Nationale, Paris.

118 The Prior of St Patrick's Purgatory locking the entrance to the church of the Cave. Miniature as p. 117 above, in Fonds Français, MS 412, Bibliothèque Nationale, Paris.

127 Pilgrim-penitent in St Patrick's Bed on Station Island, one of the drystone circles known as the Saints' Beds, which may have been brought from Saints' Island and re-erected here. The wall-plaque behind the pilgrim is illustrated in the photograph on p. 110. From *Views in Patrick's Purgatory, Lough Dearg*, 1879.

138 Detail of one of the windows by Harry Clarke in St Patrick's basilica, Lough Derg.

142 Holy well associated with St Patrick, at Cloghan Head, near Kilteel, Co. Down, from a photography by George Mott.

152 Shrine of St Patrick's bell, bronze and silver on gilt, 10th-11th century. National Museum of Ireland (as p. 38 above).

ACKNOWLEDGMENTS

The author and photographer wish to acknowledge the assistance of the Northern Ireland Tourist Board and the Prior of Lough Derg. The photograph of Croaghpatrick (6) is by Edwin Smith; the maps are drawn by Mrs Hanni Bailey.

Select Bibliography

Anscombe, Alfred, 'The Pedigree of Patrick' in *Ériu*, vol. VI, pp. 117–20, Dublin 1911. See also *Ériu*, vol. VII, pp. 13–17, 1914.

Ardill, Rev. John R., *The Date of St Patrick*, 3rd edn, Dublin 1932.

Barley, M.W., and R.P.C. Hanson *Christianity in Britain 300–700*, Leicester 1968.

Bieler, Ludwig, 'The Problem of Silva Focluti' in *Irish Historical Studies*, vol. 3, pp. 351–64, Dublin 1943.

—— 'Der Bibeltext des Heiligen Patrick' in *Biblica*, vol. 28, 1947, pp. 31–58, 235–63.

—— *The Life and Legend of St Patrick*, Dublin 1949.

—— *The Works of St Patrick*, vol. 17 of *Ancient Christian Writers*, London 1953.

—— 'Christianity in Ireland during the Fifth and Sixth Centuries' in *Irish Ecclesiastical Record*, vol. 102, pp. 162–67, Dublin 1964.

—— *St Patrick and the Coming of Christianity*, fasc.l.i., of the *History of Irish Catholicism*, Dublin 1967.

—— 'The Christianization of the Insular Celts' in *Celtica*, vol. 8c, pp. 112–25, Dublin 1968.

Binchy, D.A., 'The Fair of Tailtiu and The Feast of Tara' in *Ériu*, vol. 18, pp. 113–38, Dublin 1958.

——'Patrick and His Biographers Ancient and Modern' in *Studia Hibernica*, vol. 2, pp. 7–123, Dublin 1962.

——'The Date of the So-called Hymn of Patrick' in *Ériu*, vol. 20, pp. 234–38, Dublin 1966.

Birley, Anthony, *The People of Roman Britain*, London 1979.

Bulloch, J. B. E., *The Life of the Celtic Church*, Edinburgh 1963.

Bury, J. B., *The Life of St Patrick and His Place in History*, London 1905.

Carney, James, *The Problem of St Patrick*, Dublin 1973.

Casey, P. J. (ed.), *The End of Roman Britain*, Oxford 1979.

Certani, Rev. Giacomo, *Il Mosé dell' Ibernia, Vita del Glorioso S. Patrizio*, Bologna 1686. Translated into German, Passau 1722.

Chadwick, N.K. (ed.), *The Age of the Saints in the Early Celtic Church*, 2nd edn., Oxford 1963.

Chamberlain, George A., *St Patrick, his life and work*, Dublin 1932.

Clayton, Peter, *A Companion to Roman Britain*, Oxford 1980.

Colgan, Rev. John, *Tractatulus de Purgatorio S. Patricii*, Venice 1652.

——(ed.), *Trias Thaumaturga*, Louvain 1647.

Colgan, N., 'The Shamrock in Literature', in *Journal of the Royal Society of Antiquaries of Ireland*, 5th series, vol. 4, pp. 211–26, Dublin 1896.

Collingwood, R. G., and I. A. Richmond, *The Archaeology of Roman Britain*, London 1969.

Concannon, Mrs Thomas (Helena), *Saint Patrick, His Life and Mission*, Dublin and Cork 1931.

Cusack, Margaret F., *The Life of Saint Patrick, Apostle of Ireland*, New York 1969.

de Dartein, 'L'evangélique de'Erkambold, Evêque de Strasbourg' in *Revue d'Alsace* of 1905–6, pp. 30–33, Rixheim 1906.

de Paor, Maire and Liam, *Early Christian Ireland*, London 1958.

de Vere, Aubrey, *The Legends of St Patrick*, London 1899.

Dillon, Miles (ed.), *Early Irish Society*, Dublin 1954.

Duine, Francoise, *Inventaire liturgique de L'hagiographie bretonne*, Paris 1922.

Dümmler, E. (ed.), *Poetae Latini aevi Carolini*.

Dunn, Joseph (ed.), *La Vie de St Patrice. Mystère Breton en trois Actes: texte et traduction*, Paris 1909.

Fleming, Rev. William, Canon, *The Life of St Patrick, Apostle of Ireland*, London 1905.
—— *Boulogne-sur-Mer, St Patrick's Native Town*, London 1907.
Gogarty, Oliver St J., *I Follow St Patrick*, London 1938.
Gougaud, Dom Louis, *Les Chretientés Celtiques*, Paris 1911. English translation by Maud Joynt as *Christianity in Celtic Lands*, London 1932.
—— *Les Saints Irlandais Hors d'Irlande*, fasc. 16 of the *Bibliothèque de la Revue d'Histoire Ecclésiastique*, Louvain and Oxford 1936.
Gradwell, Monsignor Robert, *Succat, The Story of Sixty Years of the Life of St Patrick*, London 1891.
Grosjean, Rev. Paul, 'Saint Patrice d'Irlande et quelques homonymes dans les anciens martyrologes' in *Journal of Ecclesiastical History*, vol. I, pp. 151–9, 1950.
—— 'Notes d'Hagiographie Celtique' in *Analecta Bollandiana*, vol. LXIII, pp. 65–119, 1945; vol. LXX, pp. 317–26, 1951; vol. LXXV, pp. 158–226, 1957.
Gwynn, Rev. Aubrey, 'St Patrick and Rome' in *Irish Ecclesiastical Record*, April 1961, pp. 217–22.
——and R. Neville Hadcock, *Medieval Religious Houses, Ireland, with an Appendix to early sites*, London 1970.
Gwynn, E. J. (ed.), *Book of Armagh, The Patrician Documents*, Dublin 1937.
Hamilton, Rev. George F., *St Patrick and his Age*, Dublin 1932.
Hanson, Richard P. C., *St Patrick, A British Missionary Bishop*, Nottingham 1965.
—— *Saint Patrick — His Origins and Career*, Oxford 1968.
Harbison, Peter, *The Archaeology of Ireland*, London 1976.
Healy, Most Rev. John (Archbishop of Tuam), *Life and Writings of St Patrick*, Dublin 1905.
Herity, Michael, and George Eogan, *Ireland in Prehistory*, London 1977.
Hitchcock, Francis R. M., *St Patrick and his Gallic Friends*, London 1916.
Hogan, Rev. Edmund (ed.), *Documenta de S. Patricio*, Brussels 1882–98.
Hood, A. B. E., *St Patrick, His Writings and Muirchu's Life*, vol. 9 of Arthurian Period Sources, Chichester 1978.
Hughes, Kathleen, *The Church in Early Irish Society*, London 1966.
——*Early Christian Ireland: Introduction to the Sources*, Ithaca, New York and London 1972.
Jackson, H. H., *The Oldest Irish Tradition: A Window on the Iron Age*, Cambridge 1964.
Jalland, T.G., *The Life and Times of St Leo the Great*, London 1941.
Johnson, Stephen, *Later Roman Britain*, London 1980.
Kenney, James F., *The Sources for the Early History of Ireland*, vol. 1. *Ecclesiastical*, New York 1929.
Laing, Lloyd, *The Archaeology of Late Celtic Britain and Ireland, 400–1200 AD*, London 1975.
Lanigan, Rev. John, *Ecclesiastical History of Ireland*, vol. 1, 1822.
Leslie, Sir Shane, *St Patrick's Purgatory*, London 1932.
Lynch, P., *The Life of St Patrick, Apostle of Ireland*, Dublin 1928.
Mac Airt, Seán, 'The Chronology of St Patrick' in *Seanchas Ardmhacha*, vol. 11, No. 1, pp. 4–9.
MacNeill, Eoin, *Saint Patrick, Apostle of Ireland*, London 1934.
——*Celtic Ireland*, Dublin and London 1921.
——'Silva Focluti' in *Proceedings of the Royal Irish Academy*, vol. C 36, pp. 249–55, Dublin 1923.
McNeill, John T., *The Celtic Churches, A History, AD 200 to 1200*, Chicago and London 1974.
Malone, Rev. Sylvester, *Chapters towards a Life of St Patrick*, Dublin 1892.
Markus, R. A., *Christianity in the Roman World*, London 1974.
Messingham, Thomas, *Officia S. Patricii*, Paris 1620.
Mohrmann, Christine, *The Latin of St Patrick*, Dublin 1961.
Morris, Rev. W. B., *Life of St Patrick*, London and Edinburgh 1878.
Mulchrone, Kathleen, 'Die Abfassungszeit and Überlieferung der Vita Tripartita', in *Zeitschift für Celtische*

Philologie, vol. XVI, pp. 1–94, 1926.
——(ed.), *Bethu Phátraic, The Tripartite Life of Patrick*, Dublin 1939.
Nicholson, Robert S., *St Patrick, Apostle of Ireland in the 3rd Century*, Dublin 1868.
O'Connor, Daniel, *St Patrick's Purgatory, Lough Derg*, Dublin 1879.
Ó Fiaich, Rev. Tomás, 'St Patrick and Armagh' in *Irish Ecclesiastical Record*, March 1958, pp. 153–70.
O'Hanlon, Very Rev. John Canon, *Lives of the Irish Saints*, Dublin 1875.
O'Rahilly, Thomas F., *The Two Patricks, A Lecture on the History of Christianity in Fifth-century Ireland*, Dublin 1942.
O'Sulevan Beare, Philip, *Patritiana Decas*, Madrid 1692.
Oulton, J. E. L., *The Credal Statements of St Patrick*, Dublin 1940.
Pelikan, Jaroslav, *The Christian Tradition, A History of the Development of Doctrine*, vol. I, *The Emergence of the Catholic Tradition, 100–600*, Chicago and London 1971.
Plummer, Charles, *Vitae Sanctorum Hiberniae*, 2 vols, Oxford 1910.
Richardson, John, *The Great Folly, Superstition and Idolatry of Pilgrimages in Ireland. Especially of that of St Patrick's Purgatory* . . ., Dublin 1727.
Rivet, A. L. F., *Town and Country in Roman Britain*, 2nd edn., London 1964.
—— *The Iron Age in Northern Britain*, Edinburgh 1966.
—— (ed.), *The Roman Villa in Britain*, London 1969.
—— and C. C. Smith, *The Place-Names of Roman Britain*, London 1979.
Ryan, Rev. John, *Irish Monasticism, Origins and Early Development*, Dublin 1931.
—— 'The Two Patricks' in *Irish Ecclesiastical Record*, Oct. 1942, pp. 241–52.
——(ed.), *St Patrick*. Radio Éireann, Thomas Davis Lectures, Dublin 1958.
Schröder, A., *Archiv für die Geschichte des Hotstifts Augsburg*.
Seymour, Rev. St J., *St Patrick's Purgatory*, Dundalk 1918.
Shearman, Rev. John F., *Loca Patriciana: An Identification of Localities, Chiefly in Leinster, Visited by Saint Patrick . . . With an Essay on the Three Patricks* . . ., Dublin 1879.
Stanihurst, Richard, *De Vita S. Patricii*, Antwerp 1587.
Stokes, Whitley (ed.), *The Tripartite Life of Patrick, with other documents relating to that saint*, London 1887.
Swift, Edmund L., ed., transl., *The Life and Acts of St Patrick* (from the original Latin of Jocelin), Dublin 1809.
Thomas, Charles, *The Early Christian Archaeology of North Britain*, London 1971.
——*Christianity in Roman Britain to* AD *500*, London 1981.
——*Britain and Ireland in Early Christian Times*, London 1971.
Threlkeld, Caleb, *Synopsis Stirpium Hibernicarum*, Dublin 1727.
Todd, Rev. James H., *St Patrick, Apostle of Ireland*, Dublin 1864.
Todd, Malcolm (ed.), *Studies in the Romano-British Villa*, Leicester 1978.
Ussher, Rev. James, *Antiquities of the British Churches*, Chapter XVII, Dublin 1639.
Wacher, John S. (ed.), *The Civitas Capitals of Roman Britain*, Leicester 1966.
—— *The Towns of Roman Britain*, London 1974.
——*Roman Britain*, London 1978.
——*The Coming of Rome*, London 1979.
Walsh, Rev. Paul, *St Patrick*, AD *432–1932, A Fifteenth Centenary Memorial Book*, Dublin 1932.
Ware, Sir James, *De Hibernia et Antiquitatibus ejus*, London 1654.
——*Sancto Patricio . . . adscipta opuscula* 1656.
White, Newport J. D., 'Libri Sancti Patricii, The Latin Writings of St Patrick.' *Proceedings of the Royal Irish Academy*, vol. C 25, 1905, and vol. 4 of *Texts for Students*, London 1918.
—— *A translation of the Latin Writings of St Patrick*, vol. 5 of *Texts for Students*, London 1918.

—— *St Patrick, His Writings and Life*, vol. V of *Lives of the Celtic Saints*, New York 1920.

Wilson, H.A. (ed.), *The Calendar of St Willibrord*, London 1918.

Wormald, Francis (ed.), *English Calendars Before 1100*, vol. I, London 1934.

Wright, Thomas, *St Patrick's Purgatory: an Essay on the Legends of Purgatory, Hell, and Paradise current during the Middle Ages*, London 1844.

THE CONFESSIO AND LETTER

Author's translation of the Latin text of the *Confessio* and *Letter to Coroticus* is from the *Book of Armagh* collated with the six other earliest manuscript texts, of the tenth to twelfth centuries: Paris, Bibliothèque Nationale., Ms. Lat. 17626; Arras, Bibliothèque Municipale, Ms. 450; Rouen, Bibliothèque Municipale, Ms. 1391; Oxford, Bodleian Library, Ms. Fell 3 and Ms. Fell 4; London, British Library, Ms. Cotton Nero E 1.

Selected early Continental European manuscripts that include the feast of St Patrick

Calendar of St Willibrord at Echternach, early 8th century (see Bibliography, Wilson, H.A., ed.).

Calendar of Luxeuil-Corbie, 8th century (now in the Bibliothèque Nationale, Paris, Ms. Lat. 14086).

Calendar of Rheinau, 8th century; originated in Brabant, probably at Nivelles (now in the Kantonsbibliothek, Zurich, Ms. 30).

Calendar of Reichenau, 9th century; probably originated at Péronne (now in Hof und Landesbibliothek, Karlsruhe, *Codex Augiensis* CLXII).

Litanies of the Libellus Precum from Fleury-sur-Loire, 9th century (now in the Bibliothèque de la Ville, Orléans, Ms. 184).

Litanies of the Pontifical of Basel, 9th century; originated in Northern Gaul (now in the University Library, Freiburg in Breisgau).

Calendar of the Sacrementaire of Amiens, 9th century (see Bibliography, Duine).

Martyrology of Wandalbert, 9th century (see Bibliography, Dümmler, E., ed.).

Calendar of the Abbey of St Vaast, Arras, 10th century (now in the Bibliothèque Nationale, Paris, Ms. Lat. 12052).

Calendar of Freising in Bavaria, 10th century (now in the Staatsbibliothek, Munich, Ms. Lat. 6421).

Calendar prepared for Fulda or Regensburg, 10th century (now in the Vatican Library, codex 3806).

Calendar of St Maixent, Poitou, 10th century (now in the Stadtbibliothek Bern, *Codex Bengars* 441).

Litanies in the Leofric Missal, 10th century; originated in Northern France (now in the Bodleian Library, Oxford).

Litanies in the Sacrementaire of St Aubin d'Angers, 10th century (now in the Bibliothèque Municipale, Angers, Ms. 91).

Calendar of the Evangélaire of Erchembald, Bishop of Strasburg, 965–91 (see Bibliography, de Dartein).

Calendar of the Abbey of Landévennec, 10–11th century (see Bibliography, Duine).

Calendar of the Domstift of Augsburg, 1010 (see Bibliography, Schröder).

Index of Places

References in italics are plate numbers